MESSAGE FROM THE SECRETARY

I am proud to present the second Department of Energy Strategic Plan. Its publication coincides with the twentieth anniversary of the Department's creation in 1977. During the past two decades, the world has undergone many significant political, technical, and economic changes. Most recently, the government itself has embarked on a process of "reinvention" that emphasizes customer service, performance-based management, delivery of results, and accountability. These events have had major impacts on our critical mission areas and how we conduct our business operations.

With the end of the Cold War and the election of President Clinton, the Department of Energy set a new course which began with the publication of its first departmental strategic plan in April 1994. Entitled *Fueling a Competitive Economy*, it provided the framework and shared vision for meeting our responsibilities in energy, national security, environmental quality, and science and technology. The strategic plan was the guidepost for the formulation of the Department's FY 1996, FY 1997, and FY 1998 budgets and was critical to the development of the Department's Strategic Alignment Initiative, designed to save $1.7 billion over five years.

This current plan, which has been significantly improved through a very close consultation process with Congress and our customers and stakeholders, takes us to the next important performance level by being more directly linked to actions and results. It defines a strategic goal for each of the Department's four business lines and, in the spirit of the Government Performance and Results Act and the National Performance Review, identifies a fifth goal addressing corporate management. Reengineering our business practices, managing for results, being "open" with our neighbors and stakeholders, and ensuring the safety and health of our workers and the public are, and will continue to be, among the highest of our priorities. Over the coming years, we plan to achieve our strategic goals through specific identifiable strategies. Each business line has clear objectives and straightforward ways of defining whether we have succeeded in meeting those objectives.

I look forward to working with our Federal and contractor employees, other Federal, State, local, and Tribal governments, the Congress, and our customers and stakeholders to make this strategic plan a reality.

Federico Peña
Secretary of Energy

Strategic Plan

TABLE OF CONTENTS

Page

For sale by the U.S. Government Printing Office
Superintendent of Documents, Mail Stop: SSOP, Washington, DC 20402-9328
ISBN 0-16-049260-2

The Changing World

The Clinton Administration was elected with a vision for America: to move away from the Cold War economy, invest in people and technology to strengthen the economy and protect the environment, and reinvent government to become more efficient, serve the American people, and provide more services with fewer resources. This strategic plan integrates the Department's unique scientific and technological assets—including 30,000 scientists, engineers, and other technical staff at laboratories with a capital value of $30 billion—to help achieve this vision.

Each day, Americans depend on the benefits of energy, usually without considering the role it plays in our quality of life. But there have been three major oil disruptions in the past 23 years, each causing domestic and international turmoil. Furthermore, we may be entering an era of growing vulnerability to oil disruptions. By 2010, U.S. oil imports are expected to grow to 60 percent of domestic consumption, and the Persian Gulf nations will likely provide more than 70 percent of the world's oil exports, surpassing their peak of 67 percent in the embargo year of 1974.

Appreciation by public and policy makers of the interrelationships between energy production and use, and their global impact on the environment and economic growth continues to increase. DOE's energy research and development advances are being used to capitalize on the massive markets at home and abroad for sustainable energy technologies that emphasize energy efficiency, commercialization of renewable resources, safe, economic use of nuclear energy, and the economical and clean use of fossil fuels.

Electric utility restructuring has brought competition to the wholesale market under existing Federal authority, and there is considerable support, particularly among States with high electricity costs, for bringing competition to retail markets. It is not clear what the restructured industry will ultimately look like, but there will be a transition period that could last a decade or more, where the emphasis will be on profit and competitive survival.

For almost 50 years, America's national security has relied on the deterrent provided by nuclear weapons. These weapons—designed, built, and tested by the Department of Energy and its predecessor agencies—helped win World War II and the Cold War, and they remain a key component of the Nation's security. However, with the end of the Cold War there is a new set of challenges to address in the Department's national security mission. First and foremost is direction from President Clinton to DOE wherein he stated "that we can meet the challenge of maintaining our nuclear deterrent under the Comprehensive Test Ban Treaty through a science-based Stockpile Stewardship Program without nuclear testing." Additional challenges include nonproliferation, the safe dismantlement of nuclear weapons, and the disposition of surplus fissile materials. The old danger was the threat of nuclear conflict. The new danger is proliferation of nuclear weapons and other weapons of mass destruction into the hands of rogue states and terrorist groups. The United States must reduce the dangers of such weapons worldwide.

Nuclear weapons production created an enormous cleanup legacy that is, today, the world's largest environmental cleanup program. DOE is now directing the same national commitment that built the nuclear arsenal toward addressing the resulting environmental, health, and safety risks at thousands of contaminated sites. The disposal of nuclear spent fuel from commercial nuclear powerplants is another challenging problem facing the Department and the Nation. We can succeed in these endeavors only by meaningfully involving affected States and local governments, Tribal Nations, and citizens in the decision-making process, by developing new technologies to clean up sites, by demonstrating the safety of radioactive waste disposal, and by reducing future costs of long-term stewardship through new strategies for minimizing waste and preventing pollution.

Investments in research and development (R&D) have a strong influence on long-term productivity and high-wage job growth. As the United States competes in a dynamic global economy, it must lead in knowledge-based skills. This requires that both government and industry significantly invest in basic and applied science and the facilities, infrastructure, and trained workforce needed to support technological leadership. However, the relative roles of industry, academia, and the Federal government for performing R&D are undergoing significant change in the 1990s. Industry funding of basic research has declined and industry is shifting to increasingly near-term R&D, where it will result in improved short-term gains in profitability. The long-term foundations for economic productivity and technological innovation are increasingly becoming the domain of public science. DOE, with its science mission and world-class science complex and infrastructure, including the National Laboratories, is positioned well to respond to these needs.

The Changing Government

The era of big government is over. In the last few years, the President and the Congress have enacted laws and policies to reform management throughout the government. Paramount among these is the Government Performance and Results Act of 1993, which requires agencies to think of program outcomes, establish measurable annual objectives that link to long-term goals, develop budgets that are based on planned performance, and report results—beginning with the FY 1999 budget cycle and this strategic plan.

Other laws, like the Chief Financial Officers Act of 1990, Government Management Reform Act of 1994, Federal Acquisition Streamlining Act of 1994, and the Clinger-Cohen Act of 1996, call for additional management activities, products, and reports. Complementary to this legislation, the President and Vice President initiated the National Performance Review to reinvent government by focusing on results, service, quality, and customer satisfaction.

Perhaps one of the biggest challenges DOE faces is the current commitment to reducing the Federal budget deficit, which means we must fulfill our mission and deliver results more efficiently. This economic pressure requires adopting the best management, human resources, and environmental, safety, and health practices of the private sector; in other words, total quality management, defect prevention, diversity, and customer responsiveness.

The Strategic Response

Recognizing these changes in the world, and our need to change with them, led the Department in 1993 to begin a massive reshaping of our missions, priorities, and business practices. Through listening to citizens, business groups, our neighbors, and our industry partners, we agreed that dramatic change was required, not only in the Department's business lines but in how we managed our business. The result of this realization was the development and publication of the first Department of Energy Strategic Plan in April 1994. The outcomes of this initial planning effort have been far-reaching—an organization with new priorities and a sense of purpose, a new vigilance, and a culture and values that bear little resemblance to the previous organization that grew out of the Cold War.

Some examples of significant changes we have made include:

- Reforms in our management of our national laboratories, combined with reengineering at the laboratories, has allowed the laboratories to reduce administrative costs leading to expected five-years savings of over $2 billion.
- The divestiture of the Naval Petroleum Reserves, including the giant Elk Hills reserve—one of the largest government assets ever to be offered for public sale.
- The Industries of the Future program, which creates partnerships between industry, government, and supporting laboratories and institutions via a unique approach of creating an industry-driven document outlining the industry's vision for the future, and a technology roadmap to outline the technology that will be needed in order to reach their goals. Through this process, government-funded research is brought to a sharp focus to benefit U.S. industry.
- The decision to explore means other than underground testing to maintain the safety, reliability, and performance of the nuclear arsenal. This decision was based on the technical foundation and path-breaking science provided by DOE's National Laboratories to assess and certify the safety and reliability of our Nation's nuclear deterrent.
- The launch of the "openness initiative" to pull back the curtains on aspects of the nuclear age that could safely be revealed with the end of the Cold War. This ongoing initiative began with the release of information on human radiation experiments that had been conducted by the government since the end of World War II. It also includes the declassification of other significant information not requiring protection for national security, a fundamental review of DOE classification policy, the publication of a Government-wide regulation on Restricted Data classification, and the establishment of an Openness Advisory Panel to advise the Secretary on implementation.
- The development and implementation of an accelerated environmental cleanup strategy, at significantly reduced cost, with a particular focus on completing cleanup of as many DOE sites as possible by 2006. At a small number of sites, treatment will continue for the few remaining legacy waste streams. Achieving this goal requires the input and cooperation of our Tribal Nations and stakeholders.
- The remarkable cooperation with the states of the former Soviet Union to safeguard and eventually reduce quantities of weapons-usable fissile material.
- The development of an integrated comprehensive Stockpile Stewardship and Management Plan which highlights DOE's plan to meet its responsibilities under the Comprehensive Test Ban Treaty.
- Completion of a Programmatic Environmental Impact Statement for Stockpile Stewardship and Management. The Record of Decision that codified DOE's plans to rightsize the nuclear weapons complex while preserving the capabilities to maintain the nuclear weapons stockpile was signed by the Secretary of Energy in December 1996.

- Achieving major advantages in strategic computing that will enable nuclear weapons designers to perform weapons code development activities at an unprecedented rate.
- Dismantlement of 1,064 nuclear warheads during FY 1996.
- The U.S. participation in the Large Hadron Collider, reflecting the increasingly globalized perspective, high expense, and resulting need for increased international cooperation in the construction of large exploratory science facilities.
- The Contract Reform Initiative to overhaul the way work is assigned to the contractors who manage the Department's numerous laboratories and facilities. This set the stage for performance-based management contracting and enhanced competition for contract continuation.
- The Strategic Alignment Initiative to reengineer business processes and downsize the workforce to enable more to be accomplished with fewer resources and produce savings of $1.7 billion over five years.
- The formation of the Privatization Working Group to examine the best potential applications of privatization as a management tool.
- The signing of Secretarial Performance Agreements with the President for FYs 1995, 1996, and 1997 that formally identified the results the Department would deliver for its budgeted resources.

Four years of change have made a difference—we are providing better products and services, at a lower cost to the taxpayers.

This new strategic plan builds upon the knowledge and experience we have gained. We have consolidated the Department's strategic goals to five, one for each of our four business lines (Energy Resources, National Security, Environmental Quality, and Science and Technology), and one for Corporate Management that addresses improvements in our business practices and safety in all our operations. Through more tightly focused goals, objectives, and strategies, we have made the plan more action oriented by defining specific results to be delivered over the next five years. The Cold War is over—we must now face and confront the new challenges of our nation's energy, national, economic, and environmental security.

DOE's Strategic Management System

Meeting the new challenges required the Department to significantly improve its management processes. This led to the development and implementation, in March 1996, of a corporate Strategic Management System for the FY 1998 and outyear budget cycles. The system meshes the interrelated strategic planning, budgeting, and program evaluation processes throughout the Department. It provides the framework by which the Government Performance and Results Act, National Performance Review, and other financial and management legislated requirements are to be satisfied.

Performance is the common link that ties the system together. Measuring performance expands the concept of "success" from the mere accomplishment of activities to that of delivering desired outcomes and results to customers. Consistent performance measures are used throughout the processes of planning, budget formulation and execution, and evaluation.

In planning, performance is defined in terms of measurable results. In budget formulation and execution, resources are allocated and expended to deliver measurable products and services. In evaluation, success is based upon the measurement and analysis of what is actually delivered. This concept of performance is cascaded through all of the Department's organizational levels, i.e., from the DOE Corporate level down to the contractor level. Ultimately, performance measurement provides a path of accountability between the Department's long-term vision and the day-to-day activities of individual Federal and contractor employees.

The DOE strategic plan is the highest level tier of planning for the Department. It sets the strategic goals, objectives, and strategies that will be implemented through the annual performance plan, the budget, and the annual performance agreement the Secretary has with the President. The strategic goals are long-term, broad, and outcome-oriented. They are supported by objectives and strategies that are nearer-term, and, in this plan, by illustrative success measures that identify a number of representative accomplishments for the next few fiscal years. The measures for a specific fiscal year will be highlighed in the Annual Performance Plan submitted with that year's budget. Our budget requests are becoming performance-based, so the full set of performance measures are literally in the budget request. The measures contained within the annual plan will be clearly linked to the strategic goals, objectives, and strategies contained in this strategic plan.

Our Unique Capabilities

A critical step in our strategic planning process was to review our existing capabilities. What we found was that the Department of Energy has evolved a mix of core competencies that make it uniquely suited to advance science and technology, secure clean, reliable energy resources, improve the local and global environment, and reduce the nuclear danger.

The Department of Energy's roots can be traced to the Manhattan Engineer District of the U.S. Army Corps of Engineers, which was established in 1942 to manage development of the atomic bomb. After World War II, Congress created the Atomic Energy Commission in 1946 to direct the design, development, and production of nuclear weapons.

The Atomic Energy Commission was also responsible for developing nuclear reactors, and, beginning in 1954, regulating the commercial nuclear power industry. Contributions from these early efforts included isotope power sources for space missions, nuclear medicine, and high speed computers.

In 1974, Congress replaced the Atomic Energy Commission with two new agencies: the Nuclear Regulatory Commission and the Energy Research and Development Administration—the latter created to manage the nuclear weapons, naval reactors, and energy development programs, and to research the environmental, biomedical, and safety aspects of energy technologies.

In 1977, Congress created the Department of Energy, which brought together functions and responsibilities of the Energy Research and Development Administration, the Federal Energy Administration, the Federal Power

Commission, and the Power Marketing Administrations under one cabinet-level department.

The Department's unique energy-, defense-, cleanup-, and research-related responsibilities have led to distinct and singular scientific and engineering capabilities including:

- Energy and environmental technologies;
- Advanced materials development;
- Advanced manufacturing and process technology;
- High-performance computing and communications;
- High energy and nuclear physics;
- Bioscience and biotechnology; and
- Fusion plasma science and technology.

Recent accomplishments emanating from the Department's system of laboratories include:

- Nobel prizes recently awarded to DOE-sponsored scientists for pioneering work in atmospheric ozone chemistry and carbon chemistry (discovery of buckeyballs);
- Discovery, by DOE scientists, of the Top Quark, the most massive elementary particle ever seen and an important confirmation of predictions of the Standard Model of High Energy Physics;
- Development of the world's fastest computer (1 trillion operations per second), based on large-scale parallel linkages of a common computer chip;
- In partnership with industry, achievement of world-record efficiency in photovoltaic power modules using new DOE-developed thin-film technology; and

Major DOE Field Facilities

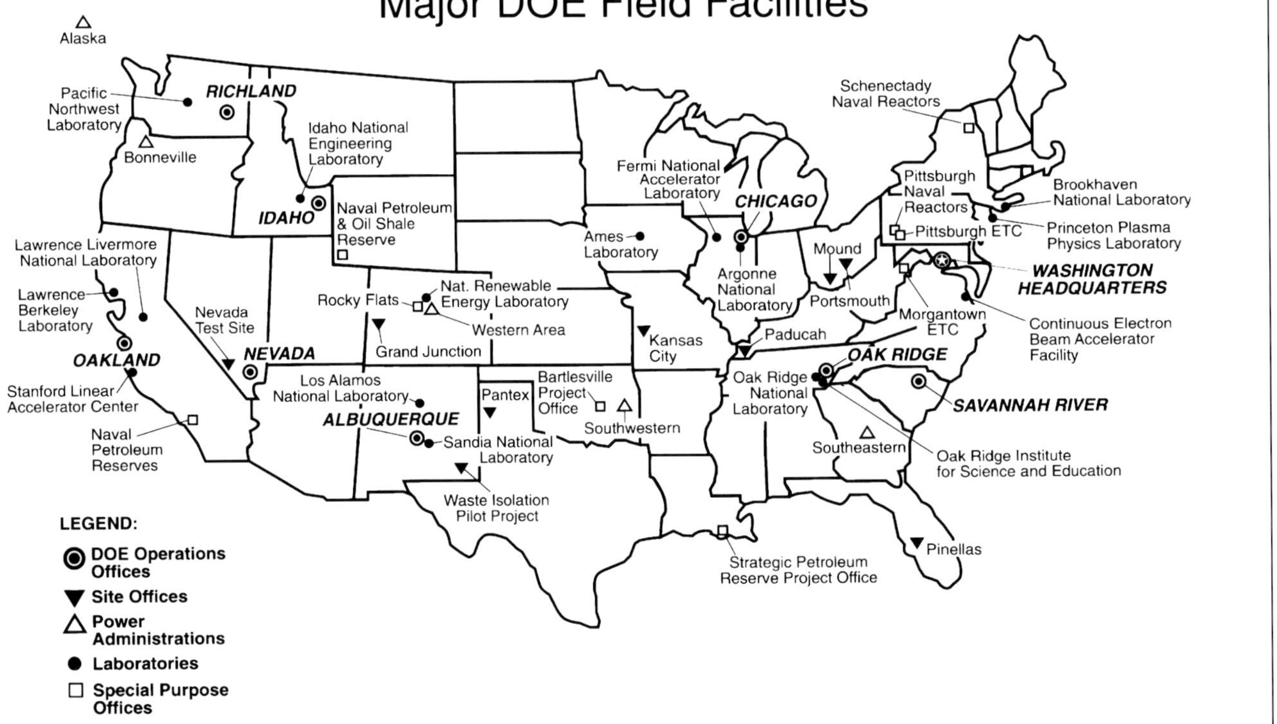

- Genome sequencing of a deep-sea, methane-producing microbe confirming the existence of a third and major new branch of life forms.

The Department has extended its basic science with a new emphasis on applied research and partnering with industry. This is best exemplified by the Partnership for a New Generation of Vehicles, a cooperative research and development agreement, negotiated with General Motors, Chrysler, and Ford to develop efficient, clean vehicles that are practical and affordable. Other examples include the sulphur light that produces four times the light at one-third the energy cost of mercury lamps; and the development of the "UV Waterworks," a technological advance that helps developing nations to quickly and inexpensively purify drinking water.

Sulfur lamp seen at dusk outside of DOE's Forrestal Building.

We are the leading Federal agency in patent applications with more than 1,500, as well as the leading agency in licenses granted with more than 400. As an example, a DOE national laboratory developed and patented an acoustic resonant ultrasound spectroscopy technology to detect defects in aircraft wheels that is now being used to determine the structural integrity of energy-related pipeline systems and bridges throughout the Nation.

In 1997, the Department's laboratories won 36 of R&D Magazine's "R&D 100 Awards" given annually for the most important inventions. This brought DOE's cumulative total to 453, twice as many as all other Federal government agencies combined.

The DOE Mission

The Department of Energy mission is:

To foster a secure and reliable energy system that is environmentally and economically sustainable, to be a responsible steward of the Nation's nuclear weapons, to clean up our own facilities, and to support continued United States leadership in science and technology.

The DOE Vision

We aspire to achieve the following vision:

The Department of Energy, through its leadership in science and technology, will continue to advance U.S. energy, environmental, economic, and national security by being:

- A key contributor to ensure that the United States has a flexible, clean, efficient, and equitable system of energy supply and end-use with minimal vulnerability to disruption;
- A vital contributor to reducing the global nuclear danger through its national security,

nuclear safety, and nonproliferation activities;

- A world leader in environmental restoration, nuclear materials stabilization, waste management, facilities decommissioning, and pollution prevention;
- A major partner in world class science and technology through its National Laboratories, research centers,university research, and its educational and information dissemination programs; and
- A safe and rewarding workplace that is recognized for business excellence, nurtures creativity, is trusted, and delivers results.

Our Core Values

The Department will succeed only through the efforts of its people. How well we perform individually and collectively is a function of the beliefs and values that motivate our behavior. The Department of Energy has chosen the following core values to serve as guide-posts and our conscience in fulfilling our mission and achieving our vision.

1. We are customer-oriented.
2. We value public safety and respect the environment.
3. We believe people are our most important resource.
4. We value creativity and innovation.
5. We are committed to excellence.
6. We work as a team and advocate teamwork.
7. We recognize that leadership, empowerment, and accountability are essential.
8. We pursue the highest standards of ethical behavior.

An amplification of these core values appears on the inside of the back cover.

Key Customer and Stakeholder Considerations

DOE will fulfill its mission through the successful delivery of its products and services to its customers and stakeholders. DOE's customers and stakeholders include the U.S. taxpayers; the energy consumers, the energy producers, the energy regulators, and the energy investors; citizens who live near DOE facilities; the businesses who work with DOE laboratories, or who are affected by their products; the family of DOE employees, laboratories, universities, contractors, and suppliers; the general science community; Federal agencies including the Departments of Defense, Transportation, Commerce, State, and Interior, the Environmental Protection Agency, Nuclear Regulatory Commission, National Science Foundation, and National Aeronautics and Space Administration; State and local governments and Tribal Nations; the Congress; the President and the Administration; foreign governments; and the news media and interest groups.

Our most important customers are the future generations, to whom we wish to leave a more prosperous and secure world.

Our customers and stakeholders have a number of concerns:

- The public demands more openness and accountability in government actions and spending. They expect more results at lower cost.

- There is concern whether the U.S. nuclear weapons stockpile can remain safe and reliable without nuclear testing.
- There is widespread national and international concern about the management and disposition of excess nuclear weapons and their components following the end of the Cold War.
- The interim storage and permanent disposal of civilian and defense radioactive waste will require more meaningful and innovative stakeholder participation than in the past.
- The public is concerned about siting new energy-related facilities close to residential areas.
- While there has been consistent public support for activities that promote environmental benefits, the public and business communities are increasingly concerned about how to reconcile economic growth and job creation with environmental goals.

Since the release of its first strategic plan in April 1994, DOE has, on an ongoing basis, greatly increased the involvement of its customers and stakeholders in its planning, budgeting, and evaluation activities. As an example, Site Specific Advisory Boards have been established at each of DOE's major cleanup sites. These boards are composed of members of environmental organizations and interest groups, the local government and business community, academic institutions, community and civic organizations, and *ex officio* members from DOE and other Federal and State agencies. The boards provide informed advice to the Department on environmental management issues, and have played a key role in the development of long-range cleanup plans.

For this strategic plan, DOE has participated in an extensive interactive, consultative process with the Office of Management and Budget and the Congress. In addition, the Department sent a draft plan for review to hundreds of other stakeholders including Federal, State and local government agencies, contractors, special interest groups, and industry organizations, and made the plan available to the general public on DOE's World Wide Web home page. All of the comments received were given consideration, and as a result, our plan has been significantly improved.

DOE's Four Businesses

Through our strategic planning efforts, we identified four business lines that most effectively utilize and integrate our unique scientific and technological assets, engineering expertise, and facilities to achieve our mission and to benefit the Nation. These business lines which directly affect the security and the quality of life of every American citizen, are:

- **Energy Resources** – How we will assure adequate supplies of clean energy, reduce U.S. vulnerability to supply disruptions, encourage efficiency and advance alternative and renewable energy technologies, and increase energy choices for all consumers.
- **National Security** – How we will effectively support and maintain a safe, secure, and reliable enduring stockpile without nuclear testing, safely dismantle and dispose of excess nuclear weapons, provide technical leadership for national and global nonproliferation and nuclear safety activities, and develop and support nuclear reactor plants for naval propulsion.
- **Environmental Quality** – How we will reduce the environmental, safety, and health risks and threats from DOE facilities and materials, safely and permanently dispose of

civilian spent nuclear fuel and defense related radioactive waste, and develop the technologies and institutions required for solving domestic and international environmental problems.

- **Science and Technology** – How we will use the unique resources of the Department's laboratories and the country's universities to maintain leadership in basic research and to advance scientific knowledge, focus applied research and technology development in support of the Department's other business lines, contribute to the Nation's science and mathematics education, and deliver relevant scientific and technical information.

Corporate Management

Working together, we recognized that for our business lines to produce results for the American people, our organizational systems needed realignment and integration. Under Corporate Management we have identified the following three areas critical to the success of our business lines:

- **Environment, Safety, and Health** – How we will ensure the safety and health of workers and the public, and protect and restore the environment.
- **Communication and Trust** – How we will communicate information and build trust within the organization and with our stakeholders and customers.
- **Management Practices** – How we will manage our workforce; allocate, spend, and account for resources; procure, produce, and contract for goods and services; streamline and continuously improve our operations and facilities; and manage our information technology systems—the tools we use to get it all done.

DOE's Strategic Goals

Working with its customers and stakeholders, the Department identified a strategic goal for each of its four business lines and one for corporate management. Each strategic goal is supported by objectives that are, in turn, supported by strategies and illustrative measures indicating progress toward accomplishing the strategies. While the goals and objectives may extend over a time horizon to the year 2010, the strategies are targeted for the next five years, and the illustrative measures are focused on FY 1998, FY 1999, and FY 2000. A comprehensive set of measures supporting the goals and objectives in this plan will be provided each year in the Department's annual performance plan and performance-based budget.

The programs that carry out the Department's goals and objectives are all within the purview of Federal Statutes, Executive Orders, and Treaties. The authorities for these programs are provided in Appendix B and are shown by business line, for each of DOE's objectives.

The following sections describe the Department's plans for each of its business lines and for its corporate management activities.

Energy Resources

A key to our Nation's prosperity has been the availability of reliable, reasonably-priced energy. The public also places a high priority on having a clean environment. Ongoing trends suggest continued domestic growth in energy use for the foreseeable future, and accelerated energy use in many developing countries. If current energy supply and use patterns persist, this growth will lead to increasing environmental emissions of global pollutants such as greenhouse gases, as well as regional and local pollutants. In addition, internationally traded, depletable resources such as oil could become more vulnerable to price and supply instability. DOE's role will be to facilitate the efficient transition to a long-term pattern of energy supply and use that is consistent with the Nation's goals of national security, environmental responsibility, and economic prosperity.

As world oil use accelerates, the Middle-East share of the export market is projected to increase. Nearer-term energy security will depend heavily on use of DOE's Strategic Petroleum Reserve to mitigate the economic impacts of short-term disruptions. DOE will also pursue a variety of oil supply, energy diversity and demand-related measures that will reduce longer-term U.S. vulnerability, as well as activities that will contribute to the reliability of the overall domestic energy system.

Energy supply, electricity production, and energy end-use have greater impacts on the environment than any other peaceful human activity, and DOE programs will be a major factor in mitigating these impacts. In the nearer-term, DOE's activities will result in cost-effective increases in efficiency and natural gas use, while new technology further reduces the environmental impacts from all fossil fuels. In the longer-term, there will be increased reliance on renewable energy, and greatly reduced environmental impacts attributable to the energy infrastructure. By resolving nuclear waste disposal issues and developing advanced nuclear technology, DOE will remove some concerns and may open the door to renewed consideration of nuclear energy as an additional option for addressing air quality and greenhouse gas emissions. DOE will also pursue technologies that could revolutionize energy supply and use, and produce major societal benefits well into the next century.

DOE, through its associations with industry and other governments, will continue to address international energy-related security and environmental concerns, and support U.S. interests in the export of advanced, clean energy technology and services. DOE will also carry out complementary non-R&D functions, including activities promoting a more efficient and environmentally sound energy infrastructure and the development of energy-related information necessary for informed consumer, market, and policy decisions. DOE will responsibly discharge its energy production and transmission responsibilities related to the Power Marketing Administrations and the Naval Petroleum and Oil Shale Reserves.

The Government Performance and Results Act stresses the depiction of outcomes in strategic plans. This has been done, where appropriate analytical tools were available[1] for a number of the strategies and measures given below. While DOE can be very successful in carrying

[1]Developing measures often involves making important assumptions, and sometimes requires the use of complex models. It is not possible to document these methodologies here, but it should be noted that unless otherwise indicated, the measures shown in this section are relative to 1996, and assume Energy Information Administration Annual Energy Outlook Reference Case Prices.

out programs that meet technical, cost, and performance goals, *the ultimate outcomes, i.e., the extent to which technologies penetrate energy markets, depends largely on the private sector.* Stressing market outcomes is important, however, to convey the potential significance of successful Federal actions in terms that are most meaningful.

STRATEGIC GOAL

The Department of Energy and its partners promote secure, competitive, and environmentally responsible energy systems that serve the needs of the public.

OBJECTIVE 1

Reduce the vulnerability of the U.S. economy to disruptions in energy supplies.

Strategy 1

Support research and development, policies, and improved regulatory practices capable of ending the decline in domestic oil production before 2005.

- *Demonstrate four advanced production enhancement technologies that could ultimately add 190 million barrels of domestic reserves, including 30 million barrels during FY 1998 and FY 1999.*
- *In FY 1999, complete with States an online environmental compliance expert system that will improve oil and gas production economics by reducing time and costs for permitting and reporting.*

Strategy 2

Maintain an effective Strategic Petroleum Reserve (SPR) to deter and respond to oil supply disruptions, and act cooperatively with member nations of the International Energy Agency

- *In FY 2000, complete the SPR infrastructure life extension program to ensure reliable operation and increase sustained drawdown capability to 4.2 million barrels per day (versus 3.7 in FY 1997) at the current fill level of 563 million barrels.*

Strategy 3

Diversify the international supply of oil and gas.

- *Continue DOE participation in international energy initiatives (such as the Binational Commissions of Russia and Ukraine, the Caspian working group, Summit of the Americas, and Asia Pacific Economic Cooperation), that are instrumental in developing, through government-to-government efforts, an effective legal and regulatory framework for private sector energy investment.*

Strategy 4

Develop alternative transportation fuels and more efficient vehicles that can reduce year 2010 projected oil (crude plus refined products) imports of 12 million barrels per day by 10 percent.

- *In FY 1999, demonstrate the feasibility of an affordable production prototype vehicle achieving 50 mpg in a hybrid propulsion, mid-size sedan.*
- *In FY 2000, startup a demonstration facility that converts low-cost waste biomass into ethanol at a production cost of $1.13 per gallon (1996 dollars) compared to $1.22 per gallon in 1996.*
- *In FY 1999, facilitate the creation of continuous corridors of alternative fuel infrastructure in and among 10 major urban centers through the Clean Cities Program.*
- *During FY 1998 and FY 1999, develop catalysts, key components, and materials for a novel gas-*

to-liquids technology that can subsequently be scaled up and tested in a process to convert remote, low-value natural gas to high quality transportation fuels and premium chemicals.

Strategy 5

Maximize the productivity of Federal oil fields, consistent with Congressional legislation.

- *By February 10, 1998, carry out the sale of the Elk Hills oil field at maximum market value.*

Strategy 6

Take measures to avoid, but when needed, respond to domestic energy disruptions.

- *In FY 1998, complete development of a modeling capability and perform analyses to guide the design of legislative options regarding reliability under electric utility restructuring.*
- *Ensure that each power system control area operated by a Power Marketing Administration receives, for each month of the fiscal year, a Control Compliance Rating of "Pass" using the North American Electric Reliability Council performance standard.*
- *Liaison with Federal, State and local governments, and private energy companies to achieve prompt restoration of energy systems following major domestic energy emergencies.*

OBJECTIVE 2

Ensure that a competitive electricity generation industry is in place that can deliver adequate and affordable supplies with reduced environmental impact.

Strategy 1

Propose legislation and support administrative actions to promote establishment of a more open, competitive electric system, with improved environmental performance.

- *In FY 1998, complete development of a modeling capability and perform analyses to guide the design of legislative options regarding electric industry competitiveness, environmental performance, and affordable customer service.*

Strategy 2

Support R&D policies and improved regulatory practices that can increase domestic natural gas supplies, moderate future price increases, and fuel 25 percent of the anticipated 6 TCF increase in natural gas demand (of which 3.5 TCF is for electricity generation) through 2010.

- *During FY 1998 and FY 1999, demonstrate 4 advanced drilling and completion technology systems that could ultimately add 6 TCF of domestic gas reserves, including 1 TCF through FY 1999.*
- *In FY 1999, demonstrate a mobile methane leak detection system with a range of at least 100 meters.*

Strategy 3

Develop renewable energy technologies and supporting policies capable of doubling non-hydroelectric renewable energy generating capacity by 2010.

- *Through primarily DOE-sponsored R&D, support the U.S. renewable industry so it nearly doubles its annual product sales of domestically produced, zero emission energy technologies to $900 million in FY 1999 compared to $500 million in FY 1996.*

Renewable energy technologies – wind power

- *Support the President's initiative to reduce greenhouse gas emissions such that the Nation will install 7,000 solar roofs in FY 1999 and 1 million by 2010.*

Strategy 4

By 2010, significantly reduce emissions from currently existing fossil fuel powerplants.

- *In FY 1999, expand voluntary industry/government collaboration to reduce greenhouse gases by catalyzing a Climate Challenge forum with over 600 utility partners to exchange lessons-learned on cost-effectively reducing greenhouse gases.*
- *In FY 1999, initiate a program to develop more accurate monitoring capabilities and identify cost-effective mitigation strategies for fine particulates (e.g., PM 2.5).*
- *In FY 1999, demonstrate commercial-scale co-firing of coal with at least 5 percent biomass.*

Strategy 5

By 2010, integrate advanced turbine and fuel cell technology to achieve market-ready gas-fueled powerplants with efficiencies over 70 percent and significantly reduced NOx compared to conventional plants.

- *In FY 1999, complete full-scale component testing of 2 advanced, utility-scale turbines with over 60 percent efficiency when used in combined cycles (new plants are currently about 55 percent) and with ultra-low NOx emissions.*
- *In FY 1999, complete testing of the first commercial-sized fuel cell module (100 KWe) using high temperature solid oxide technology suitable for advanced high-efficiency electrical generation cycles.*

Strategy 6

By 2010, reduce coal powerplant emissions by achieving market-ready coal power systems with efficiencies over 60 percent (new plants are currently about 35 percent), emission reductions less than 1/10 of New Source Performance Standards (NSPS), and CO_2 emissions 45 percent below conventional plants.

- *In FY 1999, complete commercial demonstration of one integrated gasification combined cycle project which, along with two other projects, will establish the engineering foundation leading to new generation of 60% efficient, ultraclean coal powerplants.*
- *In FY 1999, begin pilot testing of an advanced pulverized coal powerplant technology that ultimately will achieve efficiencies up to 45 percent and NOx and SOx less than 1/6 NSPS.*

Integrated gasification combined cycle coal plant

Strategy 7

Improve nuclear power plant reliability and availability to increase the capacity factor of existing nuclear power plants from the 1996 average of 76 percent to 85 percent by 2010.

- *By the end of FY 1999, identify at least three candidate advanced fuel cladding materials to support development of advanced, ultra-high burnup nuclear fuels.*
- *By the end of FY 2000, develop and demonstrate advanced balance-of-plant instrumentation and sensors in at least three plants.*
- *By the end of FY 2000, coordinate with the Electric Power Research Institute and nuclear power utilities to accelerate the Nuclear Regulatory Commission (NRC) certification of advanced digital instrumentation and control.*

Strategy 8

Maintain a viable nuclear option for future, carbon-free baseload electricity through cooperative technical development activities with U.S. electric industry that would facilitate a U.S. order of an advanced nuclear power plant by 2010.

- *By the end of FY 1998, work with industry to facilitate NRC certification of the Westinghouse AP600 design for passively safe nuclear reactors.*
- *By the end of FY 2000, design an economic data base to accurately model the schedule and cost of constructing an advanced nuclear power plant.*

Strategy 9

Develop and introduce advanced turbines that can reduce annual industrial energy costs by $500 million and carbon emissions by nearly 1.7 million metric tons in 2010.

- *In FY 1998, field test an advanced industrial turbine for 4,000 hours, and in FY 2000, complete one full-scale demonstration.*

OBJECTIVE 3

Increase the efficiency and productivity of energy use, while limiting environmental impacts.

Strategy 1

Develop and deploy vehicles, fuels, and systems of the future, contributing significantly to the Partnership for a New Generation of Vehicles to develop, by 2004, prototype mid-sized cars capable of 80 miles per gallon that will reduce NOx and CO_2 emissions by two-thirds compared to today's new car average without compromising safety, comfort, and cost.

- *In FY 1999, demonstrate the feasibility of an affordable production prototype vehicle achieving 50 mpg in a hybrid propulsion, mid-size sedan.*
- *In FY 2000, facilitate the use of nearly 500,000 alternatively fueled and powered vehicles operating in the Clean Cities and corridors.*

Partnership for a New Generation of Vehicles

CNES GOAL III

Strategy 2

By 2010, limit energy related releases of CO_2, SOx, NOx, particulates, and other wastes by as much as 5 percent relative to projected emissions by supporting R&D to improve efficiency of the Nation's energy intensive industries.

- *In FY 2000, for the seven most energy intensive industries, complete development and pursue implementation of R&D Roadmaps, where the Federal government and industry develop a strategic vision of the industry-desired future and the technology roadmap to achieve this vision.*

Strategy 3

By 2010, improve the energy efficiency of the existing U.S. building stock, and increase the energy efficiency of new homes by 30 percent and other new buildings by 20 percent compared to 1996 average new buildings.

- *In FY 1999, accelerate the market introduction of six new and emerging products that are the most efficient in their product class.*
- *In FY 1999, weatherize 77,000 homes.*
- *In FY 2000, reduce Federal energy use in buildings by 20 percent per square foot, relative to 1985.*

OBJECTIVE 4

Support U.S. energy, environmental, and economic interests in global markets.

Strategy 1

Develop policies, programs, and information to facilitate energy sector reductions in greenhouse gas emissions.

- *In FY 1998, continue to assist 18 developing countries and countries with economies in transition in developing national action plans for reducing greenhouse gas emissions and adapting climate change, and initiate assistance to an additional 2 to 3 countries.*
- *In FY 1998, promote the U.S. Initiative on Joint Implementation (USIJI) by participating in both the interagency assessment of USIJI and completing evaluations of rounds five, six, and seven of proposals submitted to USIJI.*
- *In FY 1998, complete a climate change technology strategy in partnership with private industry and top universities as part of the President's challenge to develop path-breaking technologies to address climate change.*

Strategy 2

Cooperate with foreign governments and international institutions to develop open energy markets, and facilitate the adoption and export of clean, safe, and efficient energy technologies and energy services.

- *In FY 1998, increase activities to remove barriers to U.S. companies in energy efficiency, renewables, oil and gas recovery and clean coal technology markets, in China, Indonesia, the Philippines, Brazil, India, South Africa, and the newly Independent States, and in other developing economies.*
- *By the end of FY 1998, support implementation of U.S. Government agreements with Asian-Pacific countries that open enhanced market opportunities for U.S. nuclear industrial suppliers, enabling them to exchange information and export U.S. light water reactor technology and services, contributing to a four-fold increase in U.S. nuclear-related exports (from $1.2 billion in 1997) to $4.8 billion by 2005.*
- *In FY 1999, facilitate an increase in U.S. renewable industry sales to more than $900 million (from $500 million in FY 1996), more than half of which will be exports.*

OBJECTIVE 5

Carry out information collection, analysis, and research that will facilitate development of informed positions on long-term energy supply and use of alternatives.

Strategy 1

Develop and expand public access to energy data, forecasts, analyses, and educational materials.

- *The average number of unique monthly users of the Energy Resources Board Web Sites will grow at least 20 percent per year through 2003 (from about 70,000/month in 1997).*
- *In FY 1998, complete a comprehensive national energy strategy that integrates major federal government energy-related activities.*
- *In FY 1998, publish domestic and international Annual Energy Outlooks forecasting future energy supply and consumption through the year 2020.*

Strategy 2

Carry out research and scenario analysis to help identify and understand options that could revolutionize 21st century energy markets.

- *In FY 1999, initiate a coordinated, Department-wide program to develop lower-cost, environmentally acceptable technology approaches to carbon capture and sequestration.*
- *In FY 1999, transfer fiber-optic hydrogen leak detector technology to industry (related to "hydrogen economy" concept).*
- *In FY 1999, complete analysis of test data from wells in the McKenzie Delta and offshore Carolinas to help define the volume and production characteristics of Arctic and deep marine methane hydrates.*
- *In FY 1999, complete a conceptual design study of an innovative fusion power system and evaluate the next steps as guidance to science and technology research.*
- *In FY 1999, conduct analyses to identify research needs, environmental benefits and economic factors associated with the deployment of advanced nuclear energy systems for the post-2030 period.*

National Security

The Department's national security responsibilities have traditionally been focused on matters regarding nuclear weapons, special nuclear materials, nuclear security and safety, arms control and nonproliferation, providing nuclear reactors for the U.S. Navy, and power sources for special applications. DOE is an integral part of the U.S. national security community and plays an essential role in the provision of unique technical expertise in support of the Department of Defense, the State Department, and other agencies focused on reducing the global danger from nuclear weapons, other weapons of mass destruction, and improving international nuclear safety.

Over the past several years, the United States national security policies have undergone profound change to reflect the new and evolving geopolitical military realities of the post Cold War world. Reflecting these changes, DOE has shifted its priorities toward enhancing activities which advance the Nation's nonproliferation and international nuclear safety policies while maintaining the viability of deterrence with a smaller, more agile, secure nuclear weapons complex.

The Department foresees a future national security environment with continued uncertainty and risks of international terrorism from weapons of mass destruction. In this environment, DOE is committed to a science-based program to maintain confidence in the nuclear weapons stockpile without testing, as required under the Comprehensive Test Ban Treaty. Key to the success of the science-based program is ensuring that highly qualified people are available for national security programs. DOE is also committed to safely dispose of the nuclear material made surplus by the downsizing of the nuclear arsenal in conformance with arms control and nonproliferation treaty requirements, provide nuclear reactors to the U.S. Navy, counter the proliferation of weapons of mass destruction, and further international nuclear reactor safety.

Dismantlement of nuclear warheads.

STRATEGIC GOAL

Support national security, promote international nuclear safety, and reduce the global danger from weapons of mass destruction.

OBJECTIVE 1

Maintain confidence in the safety, reliability, and performance of the nuclear weapons stockpile without nuclear testing.

Strategy 1

Extend the life of U.S. nuclear weapons by continuing the Stockpile Life Extension Program and Stockpile Maintenance activities.

- *Maintain, survey, assess, and as appropriate, refurbish specific warheads.*

Strategy 2

Improve detection and prediction capabilities for assessing nuclear weapon component performance and the effects of aging.

- *Develop, in FY 2000, additional enhanced surveillance techniques, such as improved computational models, new sensors to detect material failure, numerical simulations, and improved access to and analysis of archived test data, to assess the performance and the effects of aging for all nuclear and non-nuclear weapon components in the existing stockpile.*

Strategy 3

Continually evaluate the safety, reliability, and performance of the nuclear weapons stockpile.

- *Certify the nuclear weapons stockpile safety, reliability, and performance on an annual basis.*
- *Using two teams of experts from the weapons design laboratories, revalidate conformance to the military characteristics of the W76 warhead in FY 1999.*

Strategy 4

Provide a reliable source of tritium as required for the nuclear weapons stockpile by FY 2005 or FY 2007, depending on the production option selected.

- *Continue evaluation of the tritium production options and select the preferred option in FY 1998.*

OBJECTIVE 2

Replace nuclear testing with a science-based Stockpile Stewardship and Management Program.

Strategy 1

Develop the advanced simulation and modeling technologies necessary to confidently mitigate the loss of underground testing by FY 2004.

- *Accelerate the ongoing development of critical, full-physics, three-dimensional weapons simulation codes.*
- *Complete, in FY 1999, the installation of the three trillion operations per second Option Blue system.*

Option Red at Sandia – December 1996

Strategy 2

Develop new nuclear weapons physics experimental test capabilities.

- *Start physical construction of the National Ignition Facility in FY 1998 that will provide a means for simulating weapon-like conditions to further the study of the performance of a nuclear weapon.*
- *In FY 1998, complete the first arm of the Dual-Axis Radiographic Hydrodynamic Test Facility (DARHT) and complete design of the second arm. DARHT will provide an advanced experimental capability to validate the implosion performance of nuclear primaries.*

Strategy 3

Advance our understanding of the fundamental characteristics of weapons behavior through systems engineering and advanced experiments and modeling to support future assessments of weapons safety, reliability, and performance.

- *Annually, conduct four subcritical experiments at the Nevada Test Site to provide valuable scientific information about the behavior of nuclear materials during the implosion phase of a nuclear weapon.*
- *In FY 1998, provide full-scale engineering definition to fully certify the B61 mod 11 bomb.*
- *Provide flight test hardware for the pit reuse option for the Navy Warhead Protection Program in FY 1999.*
- *In FY 1998 and FY 1999, conduct experiments at existing facilities and compare results with theoretical models that test the flows of materials and energy that occur in weapon detonations.*

OBJECTIVE 3

Ensure the vitality of DOE's national security enterprise.

Strategy 1

Provide an appropriately-sized, cost-effective, safe, secure, and environmentally sound national security enterprise.

- *Begin, in FY 1998, the Stockpile Management Restructuring Initiative to downsize and modernize future production capabilities.*
- *In FY 1998, infuse new product and process technologies into the weapons complex through the Advanced Design and Production Technologies Program.*
- *Complete the shipment of plutonium pits from Rocky Flats to Pantex in FY 1999.*
- *Beginning in FY 1998, retain, upgrade, and consolidate the facility infrastructure to produce sufficient radioisotope thermoelectric generators to support the program requirements of U.S. government scientific and national security agencies.*
- *Demonstrate, in FY 1998, more effective safeguards and security throughout the DOE national security enterprise.*

Strategy 2

Ensure that sufficient scientific and technical personnel are available to meet DOE's long-term national security requirements.

- *In FY 1999, complete the development of a system for compiling demographic data and trends to enable management to assess the adequacy of the scientific and technical workforce.*
- *Establish strategic alliances and collaborations among the weapons laboratories, industries, and universities to enable effective use of scientific and technical personnel throughout the R&D community.*

Strategy 3

Ensure and enhance protection of nuclear materials, sensitive information, and facilities.

- *Complete, in FY 2000, ongoing improvements for deterring and defeating foreign intelligence collection against DOE technologies, expertise, and information.*
- *Initiate, in FY 1999, needed material protection, control, and accountability upgrades at DOE facilities with weapons-usable material.*
- *Further the protection of all U.S. origin nuclear materials in the U.S. and abroad from possible theft, loss, or illicit trafficking.*
- *Implement streamlined new interagency personnel security requirements in FY 1999.*
- *Upgrade the classification of certain weapons design information from Secret Restricted Data to Top Secret Restricted Data.*
- *In FY 1999, include information on nuclear materials contained in waste in a new Departmental database for all nuclear materials.*
- *Develop advanced safeguards and security technologies for initial implementation in DOE facilities in FY 2000.*
- *Initiate, in FY 1999, correction of DOE infrastructure (facilities and information) vulnerabilities identified by the President's Commission on Critical Infrastructure Protection.*

Strategy 4

Provide DOE-related intelligence and threat assessment support to members of the national security community.

- *Issue timely technical reports and threat assessments regarding potential domestic and/or foreign proliferant risks.*
- *Establish, in FY 1999, processes for the national security community to provide early warning of noncompliance with international treaties or attempted thefts and diversions of nuclear materials or nuclear warheads.*

Strategy 5

Maintain nuclear test readiness and enhance emergency management capabilities to address any nuclear weapons, radiological, or other emergency in the United States or abroad.

- *In FY 1999, complete the planning to identify and preserve the personnel skills, equipment and infrastructure needed to conduct an underground nuclear test should the President deem it necessary.*
- *In FY 1999, demonstrate and verify through exercises, improvement of a comprehensive management system to ensure Departmental response to all DOE emergencies.*
- *Demonstrate, in FY 1999, improvement of "all hazards" emergency planning and exercise activities.*

OBJECTIVE 4

Reduce nuclear weapons stockpiles and the proliferation threat caused by the possible diversion of nuclear materials.

Strategy 1

Dismantle nuclear warheads that have been removed from the U.S. nuclear weapons stockpile in a safe and secure manner.

- *Dismantle approximately 1,200 nuclear weapons in FY 1998 and 700 in FY 1999 without impacting the environment, worker and public safety, or health.*

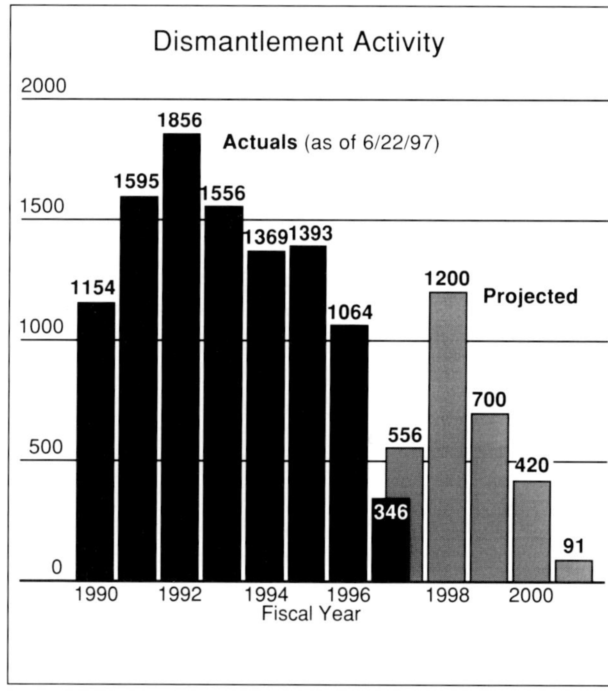

Strategy 2

Reduce inventories of surplus weapons-usable fissile materials worldwide in a safe, secure, transparent, and irreversible manner.

- *Select the plutonium immobilization technology and the sites for plutonium disposition in FY 1998, and complete the procurement for mixed oxide/irradiation services in FY 1999.*
- *Place over 20 metric tons of excess highly enriched uranium (HEU) under International Atomic Energy Agency (IAEA) safeguards in FY 1999.*

- *In FY 1999, conduct small-scale tests and demonstrations of surplus weapons plutonium disposition technologies jointly with Russia, and initiate procurement for a pilot-scale system in Russia to convert weapons plutonium to forms suitable for disposition and international inspection.*
- *In FY 1998, begin the transfer of 50 metric tons of U.S. surplus HEU to the United States Enrichment Corporation for dilution and subsequent sale.*
- *Demonstrate a prototype of an integrated plutonium pit disassembly and conversion system in FY 1999.*
- *Monitor the blending of 30 metric tons of HEU to low enriched uranium (LEU) from dismantled Russian nuclear weapons for purchase by the United States Enrichment Corporation in FY 1999.*
- *Reduce utilization of research reactor HEU through development of advanced LEU fuels by FY 2001.*
- *Eliminate weapons-grade plutonium production through reactor core conversion in the remaining three operating Russian plutonium production reactors by FY 2002.*
- *Evaluate, in FY 1999, the impacts of warhead dismantlement and transparency initiatives.*

OBJECTIVE 5

Continue leadership in policy support and technology development for international arms control and nonproliferation efforts.

Strategy 1

Strengthen the nuclear nonproliferation regime through support of treaties and international agreements.

- *Establish guidelines/requirements for global monitoring and on-site inspections to implement the Comprehensive Test Ban Treaty upon ratification by the Senate.*
- *Maintain Democratic Peoples Republic of Korea (DPRK) nuclear spent fuel in a stable, noncorrosive state through a regular inspection program while utilizing technical analysis to identify and resolve conditions that might degrade the fuel's condition prior to its transportation from the country in accordance with the U.S.-DPRK Agreed Framework.*
- *In FY 1998, participate in the interagency policy community in preparing U.S. negotiating positions for a START III.*
- *Support, in FY 1999, negotiations on the Fissile Materials Cut-Off Treaty.*
- *Strengthen cost-effective IAEA safeguards worldwide and expand IAEA safeguards to anticipate clandestine activities in potential proliferation states.*

Strategy 2

Work with the states of the former Soviet Union and others to minimize the risks of proliferation.

- *Assist the states of the former Soviet Union and others in developing effective export control policies and systems.*
- *Continue to develop United States and states of the former Soviet Union nonproliferation partnerships to redirect weapons of mass destruction expertise to peaceful commercial partnerships.*
- *Improve and integrate technology practices, facilities, and training for material protection, control, and accountability worldwide through FY 1999.*
- *By FY 2002, complete needed material protection, control, and accountability upgrades at more than 45 former Soviet Union facilities*

which use or store weapons-usable nuclear material.

- *Field, in FY 1999, an initial joint DOE-Customs Service remote inspection system capable of identifying radiation signatures of potential nuclear smuggling packages.*

Strategy 3

Advance nonproliferation technology.

- *By FY 1999, develop improved technologies and systems for early detection, identification, and response to weapons of mass destruction proliferation and illicit materials trafficking.*
- *Develop improved sensor systems for treaty monitoring and verification by FY 1999.*
- *Employ advanced technologies to provide verification confidence in FY 1999.*

OBJECTIVE 6

Meet national security requirements for naval nuclear propulsion and for other advanced nuclear power systems.

Strategy 1

Provide the U.S. Navy with safe, militarily-effective nuclear propulsion plants and ensure their continued safe and reliable operation.

- *Develop new reactor plants, including the next generation reactor, which will be 85 percent complete in FY 1999 and ensure the safety, performance reliability, and service-life of operating reactors.*
- *Ensure radiation exposures to workers or the public from Naval Reactors activities are within Federal limits and no significant findings result from environmental inspections by State and Federal regulators.*

Strategy 2

Meet ongoing and future national security requirements for special nuclear power systems.

- *Initiate a program in FY 1998 to develop a first set of advanced technology radioisotope thermoelectric generators and initiate fabrication of the first set of generators for delivery by FY 2002 and a set each year thereafter through FY 2006.*
- *Complete development of an improved thermoelectric element in FY 1998.*

OBJECTIVE 7

Improve international nuclear safety.

Strategy 1

Assist countries in reducing the risks from Soviet-designed nuclear power plants and implement a self-sustaining nuclear safety improvement program capable of reaching internationally accepted safety practices.

- *Complete the development and implementation of an effective reactor plant operator training program at key plants based on the Systematic Approach to Training methodology used in the United States and provide and incorporate plant simulators into the operator training programs in FY 1999.*
- *Provide preliminary safety assessment results to determine near-term safety improvements in FY 1998 and some final results in FY 1999.*
- *Provide, in FY 1999, Safety Parameter Display Systems to improve operator response to emergencies.*

Strategy 2

Promote nuclear safety culture improvements internationally by providing strong leadership in international nuclear safety organizations and centers.

- *Promote U.S. positions and practices in international forums that advocate safe reactor operations and effective response to radiological emergencies.*

Strategy 3

Assist in the multi-national effort to shut down Chornobyl Units 1, 2, and 3 in the Ukraine before January 2001 and reduce the risk of possible collapse of the Unit 4 sarcophagus.

- *Resolve safety issues related to inadequate heat capacity in FY 1998 and provide an adequate heat plant needed by the end of FY 2000.*
- *In FY 1998, provide Chornobyl with equipment for dose reduction, nuclear safety monitoring, dust suppression, and industrial safety.*
- *In FY 1998, reach an agreement with Chornobyl on Unit 1 defueling and before October 1999, complete a comprehensive decommissioning engineering survey of Unit 1.*

Environmental Quality

DOE is committed to honoring the Government's obligation to clean up sites across the country that supported the Nation's production of nuclear weapons, to dispose of spent nuclear fuel from civilian nuclear power plants, and to protect human health and the environment. The nuclear weapons complex generated large amounts of waste, which pose unique problems, including unprecedented volumes of contaminated soil and water, radiological hazards from special nuclear material, and a vast number of contaminated structures. Much of this massive infrastructure, waste, and contamination still exists.

The 2006 Plan, which will evolve over time to reflect stakeholder concerns, budget constraints, and technological progress, serves as the basis for much of the Environmental Quality strategic vision. We are committed to completing as much cleanup as possible by 2006 of the Department's sites contaminated from nuclear weapons research, production, and testing. Achieving our accelerated site completion goals will require DOE to improve productivity and reduce the life-cycle costs of cleanup. The geographic site completion goals in this Plan are consistent with the most aggressive budget and planning scenarios in the Environmental Management Program's Discussion Draft of the "Accelerating Cleanup: Focus on 2006" Report issued in June, 1997, and assume the maximum possible gains in efficiency. At some of these sites, these goals are extremely ambitious and represent challenges rather than specific commitments. We believe that significant cost savings and performance gains can be achieved through deployment of a large number of environmental technologies that are now at or near the end of the development pipeline. At the same time, we will use pollution prevention to reduce the Department's ongoing waste streams.

We have made significant progress in cleaning up the Department's contaminated sites. Originally, 133 geographic sites nationwide required cleanup. As of the end of FY 1996, 50 sites have been cleaned up, leaving 83 remaining geographic sites. Because completing cleanup of some of these geographic sites will not be achieved for some time, interim cleanup progress is tracked by measuring completion of key environmental activities. These include the: number of release sites completed; number of facilities deactivated and decommissioned; volume of waste treated and disposed; and quantity of nuclear material and spent fuel stabilized and/or placed into safe long-term storage. The FY 1998 and FY 1999 performance targets for some of these measures are more conservative than in the earlier draft Strategic Plan. These targets will be revised to reflect the more ambitious goals of the draft 2006 Plan as it is formulated. The revised targets will be consistent with the draft 2006 Plan and will be included in the FY 1999 Annual Performance Plan.

Even after completing cleanup, the Department will maintain a presence at most sites to ensure that the reduction in risk to human health and the environment is maintained. Such "long-term stewardship" will include passive or active institutional controls and, often, treatment of groundwater over a long period of time.

The United States also has growing inventories of spent nuclear fuel from commercial nuclear power reactors currently stored at reactor sites in 33 States, and spent fuel from nuclear-powered naval vessels. Geologic disposal is the national strategy for the ultimate disposition of this spent fuel and of defense high-level radioactive waste. It is also the technical foundation for our international stance on nuclear nonproliferation, as well as the likely path forward for other materials such as excess fissile materials. The Department has made substantial progress in characterizing Yucca Mountain, Nevada, to determine its suitability as a geologic repository site for these wastes. However, the Department continues to face substantial political opposition and legal challenges in implementing its waste disposal mandate under the Nuclear Waste Policy Act, as amended.

We must include the public, Tribal Nations, other Federal agencies, and State and local governments in decision making, with the goal of making better decisions that reflect public concerns and priorities. Key parameters such as agreements on a site's end state and the identification of required cleanup levels must be negotiated with appropriate regulators and stakeholders for each site. Additionally, we will continue to consult with our stakeholders on the proposed strategic approaches, and will incorporate public comments, as appropriate, in subsequent versions of the 2006 Plan and in the Annual Performance Plan which will implement the DOE Strategic Plan. Our environmental objectives can only be achieved through the cooperation, support, and participation of all concerned parties.

STRATEGIC GOAL

Aggressively clean up the environmental legacy of nuclear weapons and civilian nuclear research and development programs, minimize future waste generation, safely manage nuclear materials, and permanently dispose of the Nation's radioactive wastes.

OBJECTIVE 1

Reduce the most serious risks from the environmental legacy of the U.S. nuclear weapons complex first.

Strategy 1

Identify and fund projects to reduce the most serious risks first and prevent further increases in relative risk at all sites.

- *Prioritize and fund high risk projects, such that risk to the workers, the public, and the environment decreases over time.*
- *Stabilize and safely store about 100 metric tons of heavy metal of spent nuclear fuel during FY 1998 and FY 1999. This is about 5 percent of the total remaining spent nuclear fuel that requires stabilization.*

- *Stabilize and safely store more than 1,000 kilograms of plutonium at Hanford Site during FY 1998 and FY 1999.*

  Note: Plutonium data excludes information that is controlled or classified.

- *Close 2 high level waste storage tanks at Savannah River Site through FY 1999. This is about 4 percent of the tanks to be closed at Savannah River Site.*

OBJECTIVE 2

Clean up as many as possible of the Department's 83 remaining contaminated geographic sites by 2006.

Strategy 1

Accelerate and complete cleanup of 11 large geographic sites by 2006, including the Fernald Environmental Management Project, Mound Plant, Rocky Flats Environmental Technology Site, Los Alamos National Laboratory, Nevada Test Site, Portsmouth Gaseous Diffusion Plant, West Valley Site, Weldon Spring Site, Brookhaven National Laboratory, and Lawrence Livermore National Laboratory (Main Site and Site 300). Remediation progress will be measured by completion of release sites (i.e., discrete areas of contamination) and facilities (i.e., contaminated structures) that will ultimately lead to the completion of the entire geographic site.

- *Complete about 200 release sites during FY 1998 and FY 1999 for a total of over 2,400 release sites completed. This is about 60 percent of the total inventory of approximately 4,100 release sites.*
- *Decommission about 40 facilities during FY 1998 and FY 1999 for a total of over 100 facilities decommissioned. This is about 13 percent of the total inventory of approximately 750 facilities.*

Strategy 2

Cleanup the remaining 67 smaller geographic sites by 2006, including the Formerly Utilized Sites Remedial Action Program (FUSRAP) and the Uranium Mill Tailings Remedial Action (UMTRA) Project.

- *Complete surface remediation of the 8 remaining sites under the UMTRA Project by the end of FY 1998.*
- *Accelerate and complete cleanup of 4 of the remaining 23 FUSRAP sites by the end of FY 1999.*
- *Accelerate and complete cleanup of 6 of the remaining 36 other small sites by the end of FY 1999.*

Strategy 3

Accelerate cleanup at the remaining 5 large sites (Hanford, Savannah River, Idaho, Oak Ridge Reservation, and Paducah) where overall completion will not be achieved by 2006. Remediation progress will be measured by completion of release sites (i.e., discrete areas of contamination) and facilities (i.e., contaminated structures) that will ultimately lead to the completion of the entire geographic site.

- *Complete about 200 release sites during FY 1998 and FY 1999 for a total of over 730 release sites completed. This is over 25 percent of the total inventory of approximately 2,800 release sites.*
- *Decommission about 5 facilities during FY 1998 and FY 1999 for a total of over 160 facilities decommissioned. This is over 15 percent of the total inventory of approximately 930 facilities.*

OBJECTIVE 3

Safely and expeditiously dispose of waste generated by nuclear weapons and civilian nuclear research and development programs and make defense high-level radioactive wastes disposal-ready.

Strategy 1

Declare the Waste Isolation Pilot Plant (WIPP) geologic repository open for disposal of transuranic wastes in May 1998 and maximize timely shipment of waste from DOE sites.

- *Begin shipment of transuranic waste to WIPP for disposal in FY 1998 from three DOE sites (Los Alamos National Laboratory, Rocky Flats Environmental Technology Site, and Idaho National Engineering and Environmental Laboratory).*

Waste Isolation Pilot Project (WIPP).

Strategy 2

Safely and expeditiously make disposal-ready and dispose of waste generated during past and current DOE activities.

- *Dispose of about 12,000 cubic meters of mixed low level waste (MLLW) during FY 1998 and FY 1999. This is about 3 percent of the total remaining MLLW that requires disposal.*
- *Dispose of about 100,000 cubic meters of low level waste (LLW) during FY 1998 and FY 1999. This is about 7 percent of the total remaining LLW that requires disposal.*
- *Make disposal-ready (i.e., waiting for acceptance by a suitable facility) about 300 canisters of HLW at Savannah River Site and about 110 canisters at West Valley during FY 1998 and FY 1999. This is about 5 percent of the HLW remaining at Savannah River Site and about 70 percent of the HLW remaining at West Valley.*

OBJECTIVE 4

Prevent future pollution.

Strategy 1

Incorporate pollution prevention, including waste minimization, recycling and reuse of materials, into all DOE activities.

- *Reduce routine waste generation by 50 percent by the end of December 1999, based on 1993 waste generation rates.*
- *Reduce secondary waste generation from cleanup and stabilization activities by 10 percent annually, beginning in FY 1999.*

OBJECTIVE 5

Dispose of high level radioactive waste and spent nuclear fuel in accordance with the Nuclear Waste Policy Act as amended.

Strategy 1

Complete the scientific and technical analyses of the Yucca Mountain site, and if it is determined to be suitable for a geologic repository, obtain a license from the Nuclear Regulatory Commission.

- *Complete a viability assessment of the Yucca Mountain site in FY 1998.*
- *Complete a draft Environmental Impact Statement in FY 1999.*
- *Complete a final Environmental Impact Statement in FY 2001.*
- *If the site is suitable, recommend the repository site to the President in FY 2001*
- *If the site is suitable, submit a License Application to the Nuclear Regulatory Commission in FY 2002.*

Strategy 2

Maintain the capability to rapidly respond to potential statutory direction that may include transportation of spent nuclear fuel and high level waste to a designated interim storage facility.

- *Complete, in FY 1998, generic, non- site-specific interim storage facility work and address long-lead time issues related to storage of waste including design, engineering and safety analyses.*
- *Develop, in FY 1998, a market-driven approach that utilizes private sector management and operational capabilities to carry out waste acceptance, storage, and transportation services.*

OBJECTIVE 6

Reduce the life-cycle costs of environmental cleanup.

Strategy 1

Significantly enhance performance, increase efficiency and reduce costs through increased use of fixed-price competitive contracting, optimized project sequencing, recycling and other waste minimization techniques, privatization, systems engineering, and benchmarking.

- *Achieve productivity enhancement targets (Targets to be established as part of the Accelerating Clean-up: Focus on 2006).*
- *Increase the dollar value and/or number of competitively awarded fixed price contracts, including privatization contracts. (Targets to be established as part of the Accelerating Clean-up: Focus on 2006).*

Strategy 2

Develop and deploy innovative environmental cleanup, nuclear waste, and spent fuel treatment technologies that reduce cost, resolve currently intractable problems, and/or are more protective of workers and the environment.

- *The number of innovative technologies deployed. (Targets to be established as part of the Accelerating Clean-up: Focus on 2006).*
- *Costs avoided through deployment of innovative technologies. (Targets to be established as part of the Accelerating Clean-up: Focus on 2006).*

Strategy 3

Reduce operating costs by completing deactivation of surplus nuclear facilities and placing them in a safe and environmentally sound condition, requiring minimal surveillance and maintenance.

- *Complete about 100 surplus nuclear facility deactivations during FY 1998 and FY 1999. This is about 10 percent of the total remaining facilities that require deactivation.*

OBJECTIVE 7

Maximize the beneficial reuse of land and effectively control risks from residual contamination.

Strategy 1

In conjunction with stakeholders, develop comprehensive land use plans for DOE sites that provide information on alternative uses, ownership, environmental requirements, and implementation schedules.

- *Submit to Congress future use plans for the Hanford Site, Savannah River Site, Rocky Flats Environmental Technology Site, and Idaho National Engineering and Environmental Laboratory by May 1998.*
- *Develop future use plans for all other major DOE sites in conjunction with stakeholders.*

Science and Technology

Science and technology have been the cornerstones for U.S. economic strength for well over a century and are expected to be even more important to the Nation's economy in the future global market. Publicly-funded science and technology in support of various agency missions have been a major, if not the dominant, contributor to the scientific knowledge base and continuing revolutionary breakthroughs responsible for sustained U.S. economic prosperity, and other quality of life benefits.

DOE is one of the top five agencies that are major providers of science and technology to the Nation. DOE maintains a unique role in the science community with its focus in such areas as:

- High energy and nuclear physics, exploring the fundamental nature of energy and matter;
- Biological and environmental research, supporting energy options, climate change issues, and DOE facility operations;
- Basic energy sciences that encompass materials, chemicals, biotechnology, geosciences and other research disciplines essential to the development of new, more promising energy options;
- Fusion energy sciences, encompassing plasma and supporting sciences;
- Advanced computing and technology research in support of physics, fusion, and other DOE programs, and linking DOE online with the broader science community;
- Fossil energy research supporting goals to enhance the discovery, recovery, and clean and efficient use of a diverse set of fossil fuels;
- Energy efficiency research, including conservation and renewable energy research;
- Nuclear energy research, including advanced nuclear power systems to support various National Aeronautics and Space Administration (NASA) missions, and research into the production and use of new isotopes;
- National security research that supports nuclear stockpile stewardship and research that supports international nuclear detection and nonproliferation objectives; and
- Environmental cleanup research that addresses the complex waste products and cleanup needs at the Department's field sites.

DOE works closely with other Federal agencies to tackle the major scientific and technological challenges facing the Nation. DOE brings to the table a vast array of mission-related capabilities through its National Laboratories, world-class research performers, and advanced scientific user facilities that each year provide access to many thousands of industry, university, and government (e.g. other agency) scientists.

DOE's Science and Technology business line is focused on four areas: 1) science and basic research; 2) energy, national security, and environmental technology development; 3) management of DOE's research enterprise, including facilities and infrastructure; and 4) a modest, but important supporting role in helping to meet the Nation's math and science education goals.

STRATEGIC GOAL

Deliver the scientific understanding and technological innovations that are critical to the success of DOE's mission and the Nation's science base.

OBJECTIVE 1

Develop the science that underlies DOE's long-term mission.

Strategy 1

Conduct relevant, high quality, innovative research that responds to the needs of the DOE mission.

- *Maintain the high quality and relevance of DOE's science as evaluated by annual peer reviews and advisory committees.*
- *Complete sequencing of forty million subunits of human DNA for submission to publicly accessible databases in FY 1999.*

Decoding human genome

- *Complete the genetic sequencing of more than 10 new microbes in FY 2000, doubling the total number completed by the scientific community to date, and focusing on those with significant implications for waste cleanup and energy production.*
- *Increase the number of newly characterized macromolecular structures from 50 per year in FY 1997 to 150 per year in FY 2000, in structural biology experiments at DOE-supported user-facility synchrotrons.*
- *Complete clinical trials of Boron Neutron Capture Therapy for at least 50 patients in FY 1998.*
- *Maintain maximum operating schedules for all major scientific-user facilities (advanced scientific facilities made available to the general science community), including operations for applicable facilities at levels established by the Scientific Facility Initiative.*

- *Complete preparations for the start of construction for the National Spallation Neutron Source in FY 1999*
- *Reach transmission speeds of over one billion bits per second on the nationwide Energy Science Network (ESnet) in FY 2000, enhancing scientific collaborations over the Internet.*
- *Achieve sustained processing and calculational speeds of two trillion operations per second for application in a global climate change model.*
- *Achieve readiness for operation of the National Spherical Tokamak Experiment at the Princeton Plasma Physics Laboratory in FY 2000.*
- *Answer critical scientific questions in FY 2000 surrounding the basic physical and chemical properties of various mixed chemical and highly radioactive wastes stored in over 300 storage tanks across the Department.*
- *Compile information on lightning and the structure of the ionosphere in FY 2000 in connection with the satellite-based electromagnetic pulse sensor demonstration*

Strategy 2

Provide new insights into the fundamental nature of energy and matter.

- *Maintain the high quality and relevance of DOE's science as evaluated by annual peer reviews and advisory committees.*
- *Complete preparations and begin operation in FY 1999 of the B-factory at the Stanford Linear Accelerator Center and the Tevatron at Fermilab (with the newly completed main injector).*
- *Commence full research at the Relativistic Heavy Ion Collider in FY 2000 to set the stage to observe possible evidence of the predicted quark-gluon plasma—a state of nuclear matter believed to have existed one millionth of a second after the "Big Bang."*

Fermilab

- *Commence full operation in FY 1998 of all 3 experimental halls at the Thomas Jefferson National Accelerator Facility to explore the structure of atomic nuclei.*
- *Begin experimental data-taking in FY 2000 to resolve the fundamental issue of whether neutrino particles have mass—an important issue for high energy and nuclear physics understanding.*

Strategy 3

Search for and utilize the best talent from all sources to perform DOE research.

- *Increase the already extensive amount of research committed to open, competitive solicitations through FY 2000.*
- *Increase the weight of proposal evaluation criteria that emphasize the scientific excellence of performers independent of organizational affiliation.*

Strategy 4

Develop science to support DOE's participation in energy and other National policy formulations.

- *Complete development of the next generation climate model in FY 2000.*

Strategy 5

Support emerging sciences that are important to the future of DOE and the Nation, including interdisciplinary research that addresses the Nation's most pressing problems.

- *Increase the number and extent of collaborations with others on complex problems, such as climate change and fuel-efficient vehicles, that require interdisciplinary research capabilities.*
- *Streamline processes in FY 1998 for entering into interagency agreements for emerging interdisciplinary research.*

Strategy 6

Leverage research opportunities through science partnerships and pursue international science collaborations.

- *Sign, in FY 1998, the international agreement to participate in the construction and management of the Large Hadron Collider accelerator and the two major detectors.*
- *Complete, in FY 1998, the memorandum of understanding with the National Science Foundation concerning the management of the U.S. Large Hadron Collider activities.*
- *Complete evaluation of the readiness to proceed with International Thermonuclear Experimental Reactor construction with other parties in FY 2000.*
- *Complete review of proposals and initiate projects in FY 1998 to design and develop advanced catalysts, electrodes, and membranes, as well as advanced separator plates and high temperature sealants under the Russian-American Fuel Cell Consortium.*
- *Increase annually the number of domestic science partnerships and the leverage of DOE research dollars through FY 2000.*

OBJECTIVE 2

Deliver leading-edge technologies that are critical to the DOE mission and the Nation.

Strategy 1

Develop the technologies required to meet DOE's energy, national security, and environmental quality goals.

- *Validate, in FY 2000, new DOE technologies that deliver benefits faster, better, and cheaper than existing technologies.*
- *Achieve increased national recognition for accomplishments through National R&D 100 and equivalent awards.*
- *In FY 1999, expand the use of risk assessments, cost-benefit analysis, and other analytic tools in setting technology R&D priorities.*
- *Enhance tomographic and other imaging technologies in FY 1999 with an overall goal of aiding industry to find an additional 4 billion barrels of oil.*

Atmospheric radiation measurement at PNNL.

- *Demonstrate the appropriate biotechnology in FY 1999 to upgrade heavy oil and residues using microbes that preferentially remove organically bound sulfur, nitrogen, and heavy metals.*
- *Initiate development of highly efficient radioisotope power systems in FY 1998 in support of NASA's future mission requirements.*
- *Supply quality stable and radioactive isotopes for industrial, research, and medical applications that continue to meet customer specifications and maintain 95 percent on-time deliveries in FY 1998 and beyond.*
- *Develop new isotopes for industrial, research, and medical applications, including a domestic capacity to produce a reliable supply of the vital diagnostic isotope molybdenum-99; alpha-emitting isotopes; and short-lived accelerator radioisotopes to be used in human clinical trials in FY 2000.*
- *Complete construction and commissioning of the Los Alamos Target Irradiation Station in FY 2000 to improve isotope quality with greater operating efficiency.*
- *Develop and prove technologies in FY 2000 that will result in the permanent safe closure of high level waste tanks across the DOE complex.*
- *Validate performance of thermal and non-thermal treatment technologies in FY 2000 for the treatment of more than 90 percent of the DOE mixed waste inventory.*
- *Develop technologies that reduce the cost to characterize and treat heavy organic liquids and radioactive metals in the subsurface by 50 percent over conventional pump and treat options.*
- *Develop and deliver the next generation space-based nuclear treaty monitoring sensors to the Air Force for launch in FY 2000.*
- *Develop and deliver to the Air Force for launch in FY 1999 a small DOE satellite that demonstrates multi-spectral thermal imaging technology for detecting nuclear proliferation.*

Strategy 2

Pursue technology research partnerships with industry, academia and other government agencies and proactively accelerate the transition of technologies to end users.

- *Build on this year's interagency participation in DOE's science and technology strategic planning, to expand interagency participation and expand linkages to the National Science and Technology Council during the next planning cycle.*
- *Increase the number of partnerships through FY 2000.*
- *Increase the total dollars leveraged through FY 2000.*
- *Implement innovative funding options in FY 2000 for research and development activities*
- *Increase the number of demonstrated feasible technologies that are commercialized by the private sector through FY 2000.*
- *Increase the aggregate estimate of benefits of technologies introduced through FY 2000.*
- *Increase the number of new technologies field tested and used at DOE facilities in FY 1999.*

OBJECTIVE 3

Improve the management of DOE's research enterprise to enhance the delivery of leading-edge science and technology at reduced costs.

Strategy 1

Manage the National Laboratories, science-user facilities, and other DOE research providers and research facilities in a more integrated, responsive, and cost-effective way, building on unique core strengths and corresponding roles

- *Reduce the cost of performing research by reducing the administrative burdens on the laboratories and through laboratory reengineering.*
- *Map capabilities, core strengths, and leadership roles across the DOE research enterprise in FY 1998.*
- *Implement a review process to ensure programmatic decision-making is consistent with mapping in FY 1998.*
- *Complete prototype development of the "virtual lab" approach and implement in several program trial applications in FY 1999.*
- *Field test new computational and communication technologies that improve linkages in operations and operate three experimental user facilities remotely over the ESnet in FY 2000.*
- *Through FY 2000, improve science-technology integration by increasing the percentage of Department projects that undergo up-front coordination by all members of the innovation pathway, i.e., basic researchers, technology developers, and implementors defining needs together.*
- *Increase the ratings of user-facility satisfaction as determined by periodic customer satisfaction surveys.*

Strategy 2

Design, construct, and operate research facilities in a timely and cost-effective manner.

- *Benchmark, in FY 1999, national and international performance in the design, operation, construction cost, and schedules of large research facilities.*
- *Develop and validate, in FY 2000, innovative technical approaches to address scale-up size and cost issues posed by the next generation of science facilities.*

Strategy 3

Improve the management, dissemination, sharing, and use of scientific and technical information across DOE

- *Complete the remaining 30 percent of a DOE-wide database of ongoing research and development in FY 1998.*
- *Make established scientific journals electronically available at the desktop in FY 1999.*

Strategy 4

Improve peer and program review processes.

- *Increase the coverage and improve the quality of peer reviews in FY 1999.*
- *Conduct a review on the peer and program review processes and implement recommendations in FY 1999.*

OBJECTIVE 4

Assist in the government-wide effort to advance the Nation's science education and literacy.

Strategy 1

Develop and promote technologies and programs that deliver information and contribute to learning in science, math, engineering and technology, and in general, expand access to DOE's technical information.

- *Demonstrate increased public access to DOE technical information on an annual basis starting in FY 1998.*
- *Improve ratings contained in periodic customer satisfaction surveys of DOE's information and outreach programs starting in FY 1999.*
- *Develop and extend the use of Internet-based Hands on Science Laboratories in FY 1999.*

Strategy 2

Leverage DOE's human and physical research infrastructure, working with the National Science Foundation and other Federal agencies, to promote science awareness, enable advanced educational research opportunities, build capabilities at educational institutions, and improve educational opportunities for diverse groups.

- *Expand sponsorship of collaborations for local and regional science awareness events starting in FY 1998.*
- *Demonstrate increased opportunities for undergraduate and graduate student research at DOE labs and other facilities through FY 2000.*
- *Retain a greater number of student interns for subsequent employment in DOE's research enterprise in FY 2000.*
- *Demonstrate an annual increase in the diversity of DOE research performers through FY 2000.*

Corporate Management

The Department recognizes that the key to its success rests in corporately managing its diverse portfolio. With this in mind, DOE will utilize strategic planning and budgeting, performance plans and agreements, and additional corporate-minded approaches and systems to guide Departmental activities and decision-making. We will continually look across programmatic and operational lines, establish priorities and prudently allocate resources, and achieve intended business-like results efficiently and cost-effectively. This corporate mind-set will allow us to further reduce costs and red-tape, empower our front-line employees to get the job done, and make the most of our available resources while providing our customers and stakeholders with the highest quality products and services that they demand.

While corporate management traditionally includes the administrative, staff, and operational functions of an organization; at the Department of Energy it also involves integrating into everything we do a genuine concern for the environment, safety, and health of our workers and the public; effective communication and trust with our customers and stakeholders; and highly efficient management practices. While much progress has been made in these areas over the last four years, we still have further to go if we are to be recognized as a good neighbor, an effective stakeholder and customer partner, and a world-class quality organization.

Since the Department has stewardship over some of the most hazardous materials known to mankind, our safety and health concerns and environmental problems are formidable. This requires a level of vigilance commensurate with the danger. Protecting our workers and respecting the health and safety of our neighboring communities will be among our highest priorities. We are shifting from a reactive approach to environment, safety, and health matters, to one that emphasizes prevention. All departmental businesses are proactively ensuring that there is no compromise to public and worker safety and health, and that every effort is made to minimize the generation and release of wastes and pollutants into the environment.

The Department has undergone a transformation from a secretive, weapons-producing agency; little understood outside of Washington; to a results-driven, customer-focused leader in science, technology, and environmental management. This change in culture has been accomplished by emphasizing openness, enhancing communications, and fostering trust. Our commitment to an open and accountable government will continue and be strengthened through the actions outlined in this plan. As such, we will work in partnership with our customers and stakeholders to establish priorities and measure results.

By focusing on management issues, the Department has made significant progress aligning resources with agency priorities, streamlining operations, and reducing costs. Gender, ethnicity, age, and skills diversification have brought new thinking and perspectives that heretofore have not had a voice in departmental decision-making. We are challenged, however, to maintain this progress in the face of continually shrinking budgets. As the workforce is reduced, special care must be given to protecting Departmental advancements in a wide range of programmatic and functional areas.

As envisioned in the Blair House Papers, the Department will continue to be a significant contributor to the Administration's deficit reduction objectives. Savings will result from the realignment of the Department's mission priorities, its focus on customer service and total quality management, contract reform and privatization, and its leadership role in support of the reinventing government initiative.

Wherever practicable, the best in private sector business practices will be utilized. Greater competition, transparent performance and outcome-based budgets and contracts, and a dedication to reengineering systems and processes will continue as a part of the Department's new corporate management paradigm. In short, we intend to continue to achieve greater results at less cost to the American taxpayer.

STRATEGIC GOAL

The Department of Energy continuously demonstrates organizational excellence in its environment, safety and health practices, communication and trust efforts, and its corporate management systems and approaches.

OBJECTIVE 1

Ensure the safety and health of the DOE workforce and members of the public, and the protection of the environment in all Departmental activities.

Strategy 1

Integrate and embed sound environment, safety, and health (ES&H) management practices into the performance of DOE's day-to-day work.

- *Prevent fatalities, serious accidents, and environmental releases at Departmental sites.*
- *Implement Integrated Safety Management Systems at DOE's 10 priority facilities and in all major management and operations contracts in FY 1999.*
- *Clarify ES&H roles and responsibilities through the issuance of Functions, Responsibilities, and Authorities Manuals for the Secretarial Officers and for the Department's sites associated with the 10 priority facilities by October 1997. The remaining Secretarial Officers and all appropriate national security-related and non-national security-related sites will issue safety management roles and responsibilities documents by July 1998.*
- *Conduct annual self-assessments at all DOE sites to identify ES&H deficiencies and vulner-*

abilities, and develop and pursue corrective action plans.

- *Provide expanded access to information on health related risks from operating our facilities to ensure that minority and low-income populations which may be disproportionately adversely impacted by DOE facilities understand the Department's environmental justice goals and strategies.*

Strategy 2

Clearly identify and fund ES&H priorities and ensure resources are appropriately spent on those priorities.

- *Conduct sufficient workscope planning and identify and fund ES&H priorities in the FY 1999 budget and annually thereafter.*
- *Starting in October 1997, annually monitor and report on ES&H expenditures and improve related internal controls.*

Strategy 3

Ensure that all DOE employees are appropriately trained and technically competent commensurate with their ES&H responsibilities.

- *Meet annual DOE Technical Qualification Program goals for personnel whose responsibilities impact safety at current and former defense nuclear facilities.*
- *Ensure employees that perform physically hazardous work and activities at non-defense facilities meet or exceed competency requirements.*

Strategy 4

Work with the Nuclear Regulatory Commission and the Occupational Safety and Health Administration to evaluate the costs and benefits of independent external regulation of safety and health.

- *Initiate three pilot projects for independent external regulation during FY 1998.*

OBJECTIVE 2

As a good neighbor and public partner, continually work with customers and stakeholders in an open, frank, and constructive manner.

Strategy 1

Foster strong partnerships with neighboring DOE communities, regulators, and other stakeholders to determine priorities and solutions.

- *During FY 1998 and FY 1999, charter intergovernmental working groups to annually review and/or update programmatic and ES&H data and communicate findings to the public.*
- *Establish a structured forum at each Field site in FY 1999 to involve customers and neighboring communities in DOE decision-making.*

Strategy 2

Increase customer and public awareness of DOE's mission areas by improving the quality, timeliness, frequency, and sufficiency of information disseminated on the Department's functions, successes, lessons learned, and future activities.

- *During FY 1998 and FY 1999, reduce the Freedom of Information Act backlog by 15 percent and the average case age by 25 percent.*
- *Annually improve the quality and volume of information on DOE's World Wide Web site and demonstrate user-interest through higher numbers of home page visits each year.*
- *Publish, during FY 1998, a comprehensive document that clearly identifies the roles, responsibilities, assignments, authorities, and account-*

abilities of Headquarters, Field, and Contractor organizations and staff.

- *Continually provide the Office of Management and Budget and Congress with timely, sufficient, and accurate information to enhance collaboration and decision-making.*

Strategy 3

Increase openness with the public by prudently declassifying information about the Department's activities while maintaining a balance with the Nation's security.

- *Review thousands of DOE documents during FY 1998 and FY 1999 for possible declassification and release those that no longer need to be withheld for security purposes.*
- *Implement, in FY 1999, over 70 interagency coordinated declassification actions related to interagency documents containing substantial amounts of nuclear weapons-related information.*
- *In FY 1999, implement 10 CFR 1045 through reviewing 10 percent of other agency classification guides as well as reducing and improving 20 percent of DOE's own classification guides.*

OBJECTIVE 3

Use efficient and effective corporate management systems and approaches to guide decision making, streamline and improve operations, align resources and reduce costs, improve the delivery of products and services, and evaluate performance.

Strategy 1

Improve decision-making, ensure accountability, maximize departmental resources, and achieve intended results by corporately managing the Department's mission, functions, and activities.

- *Utilize, during FY 1998, mechanisms such as senior level corporate and business line management councils, a DOE chief operating officer, and performance-based management to foster strategic direction, enhance programmatic integration, and improve headquarters and field operations.*
- *Develop annual performance-based budgets by using DOE's corporate Strategic Management System that links resource requirements to five-year plans, independent project validations, and cross-cutting program evaluations.*
- *Establish, by December 1997, annual Secretarial Officer Performance Agreements that are linked to the Secretary's Performance Agreement with the President.*
- *Utilize, by December 1997, an off-the-shelf Executive Information System to provide senior management with timely cost, schedule, and performance data.*

Strategy 2

Use prudent contracting and business management approaches that emphasize results, accountability, and competition; improve timeliness; minimize costs; and ensure customer satisfaction.

- *Convert all existing management and operating contracts to performance-based management contracts (performance objectives and measures) as they are either extended or competed, and award 50 percent of support service contracts as performance-based by the end of FY 2000.*
- *By September 1998, increase the number of competitively awarded contracts for major DOE sites and facilities from 13 to 16.*
- *Annually identify and pursue privatization opportunities, and during FY 1998, hire a DOE privatization director and develop a Department-wide privatization strategy.*

- *Apply business process reengineering to the highest priority procurement processes by September 1998 with a goal of reducing cycle time by 30 percent.*
- *Improve Federal procurement and property management employee skills by establishing a contracting workforce development program by September 1998*
- *Implement, by September 1998, an automated system to track and measure contractor performance.*

Strategy 3

Continue to streamline and improve operations, further reduce overhead expenditures, and facilitate additional workforce reductions while aiding affected employees and communities

- *Realize annual Strategic Alignment Initiative savings commitments totaling $1.7 billion by the end of FY 2000.*
- *Meet the Department's annual Federal and contractor staff reduction targets through FY 2000, in accordance with budget agreement targets.*
- *Implement, during FY 1998, the necessary systems to track and report on major DOE cost-savings commitments such as a single Department-wide automated contractor workforce employment data system.*
- *Annually hold to two percent or less the outside hiring for contractor positions vacated through voluntary incentive programs or involuntary separations.*
- *Ensure reemployment of at least 60 percent of separated contractor workers seeking new jobs in equivalent positions within 2 years of separation.*

Strategic Alignment Initiative

SAI Commitment to Save $1.7 Billion by the end of Fiscal Year 2000

- **Federal Staffing** – Reduce DOE staffing by 3,788 federal employees, (27%); saving $810 Million over 5 years.
- **Support Contractor Savings** – Reduce support services by a total of $450 Million (13%) over 5 years.
- **Information Management Savings** – Cut IRM expenses by $245 Million (5%) over 5 years through better systems, large scale procurements and eliminating redundancies.
- **Travel Savings** – Reduce Federal and contractor travel costs by $175 Million (11%), or $35 Million per year.
- **National Environmental Protection Act Savings** – Streamline NEPA processes to save a total of $26 Million (20%) by FY 2000.
- **Asset Sales** – Sell no longer needed assets such as precious metals and specialized machinery to save (return to Treasury) $75 Million by FY 2000.

- *Support local community transition activities that will create 10,000 to 15,000 new private sector jobs by the end of FY 1999.*

Strategy 4

Implement quality management principles, value diversity, and continue to improve human resources systems and practices.

- *Improve workforce skills and reduce training costs by establishing two Training Centers of Excellence by December 1997.*
- *Hire 55 Welfare-to-Work recipients by the end of FY 1998.*
- *By December 1998, implement a DOE-wide employee accessible automated personnel system and reengineer at least one Personnel/Training process in both FY 1998 and FY 1999.*
- *In FY 1999, maintain workforce diversity at FY 1997 levels or better, provide at least 10 percent of DOE's education grants to minority institutions, and award at least 20 percent of the Department's contracts to small and minority businesses.*
- *Expand the use of Alternate Dispute Resolution during FY 1998 and FY 1999 by 30 percent to mediate workplace disputes such as Equal Employment Opportunity complaints and grievances.*
- *Using the Malcom Baldrige, President's or Energy Quality Award Criteria, demonstrate continuous organizational improvement by achieving self-assessment scores of at least 300 in FY 1998 and higher scores in subsequent years.*

Strategy 5

Strengthen the management of projects, materials, facilities, land, infrastructure, and other assets, to ensure safe, sound, and cost-effective operations, appropriate maintenance of sites, and to ensure intended project results.

- *Annually meet established project scope, schedule, and cost baselines by adopting systems based on industry and government best project management practices.*
- *Implement, in FY 1999, a risk-based site priority system to enhance the ability of field sites to plan, budget, and track performance of new and existing infrastructure requirements.*
- *Conduct annual business management self-assessments to ensure that sites are maximizing their resources and maintaining safe and secure operations.*
- *Return to the Treasury at least $15 million annually through the sale, transfer, re-use, or disposal of unneeded materials, facilities, land, and other assets.*

Strategy 6

Utilize, under the auspices of the Chief Information Officer, an integrated Department-wide framework for planning, budgeting, evaluating, and implementing information management requirements to reduce costs and improve operations.

- *Establish, by October 1997, the Capital Planning Information Technology Investment Board and operationalize the requirements of the Clinger-Cohen Act of 1996.*
- *Starting in FY 1998, implement a five-year information management plan and produce annual operational plans as part of the Department's budget process.*
- *Implement, by January 1998, a Department-wide information architecture with supporting standards to foster $100 million in cost avoidances over the next 5 years.*
- *Provide the necessary infrastructure by December 1999 to allow staff the capability of accessing and sharing information easily and seamlessly across the DOE complex.*

Resource Requirements

The Department will only achieve its goals and objectives with adequate financial, human, infrastructure, and technical resources. In developing this plan, the Department assumed budget appropriations consistent with the Administration and Congress's agreed upon five-year budget deficit reduction targets through FY 2002.

Federal staffing levels are based upon the Department's Strategic Alignment Initiative targets (that do not include the Federal Energy Regulatory Commission and the Power Marketing Administrations) established in 1995. These targets call for an overall Federal staff reduction of 27 percent by FY 2000 to a level of 10,269. In addition, DOE will reduce contractor staffing levels to 91,000, a 38 percent reduction from the peak level of 148,686 in FY 1992. Any further decreases in these budget or staffing levels will adversely impact the Department's ability to meet its commitments.

The Department recognizes some additional future initiatives for which resource availability must still be resolved. Examples of these special programmatic needs are identified below.

In the National Security area, replacing nuclear testing with a science-based stewardship and management program will require development of advanced experimental and computational capabilities and a shift in workforce skills from nuclear weapons design, testing, and analysis to modeling, simulations, and systems analysis. The loss of nuclear expertise

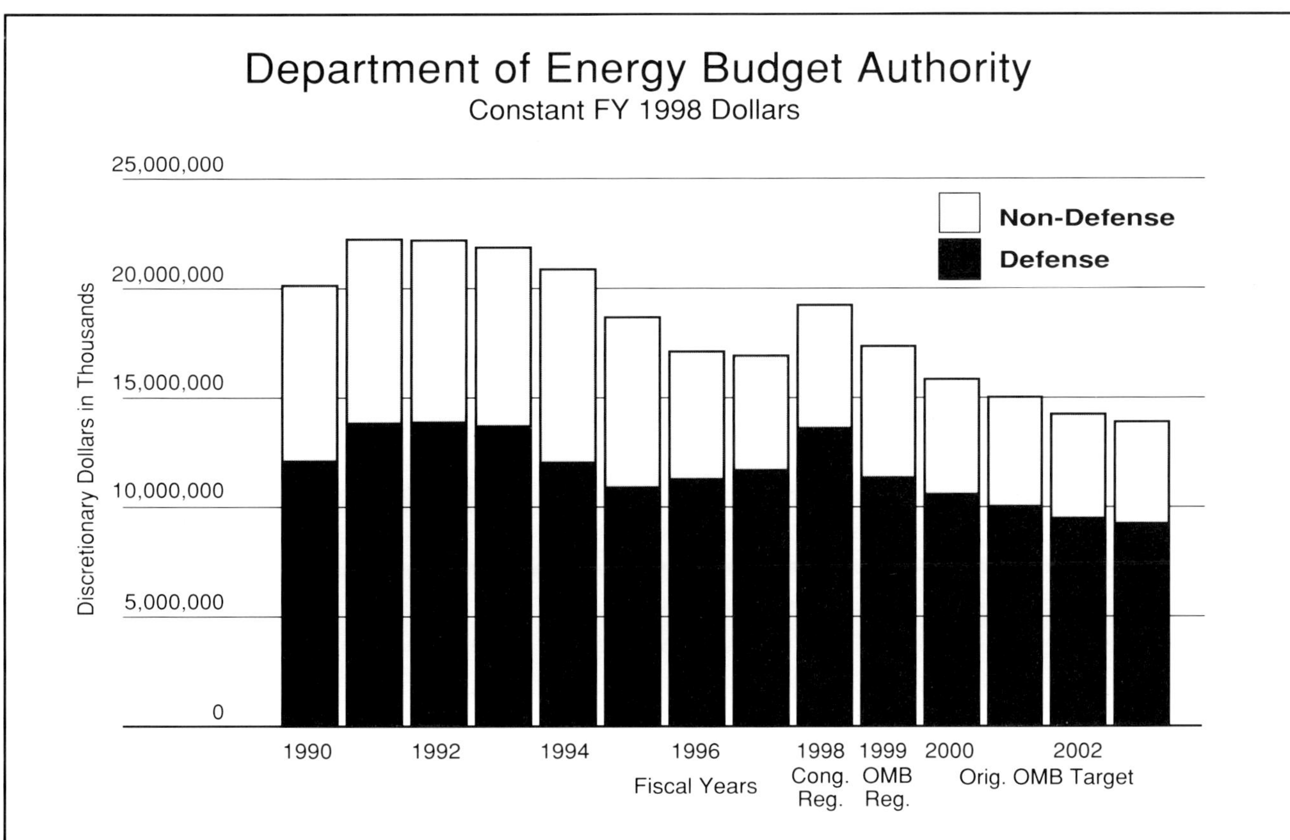

Strategic Alignment Initiative
Federal Staffing Reductions – Exceeding Alignment Goals
(Does not include Power Marketing Administrations and Federal Energy Regulatory Commission)
Strategic Alignment Plan
Actual Employment
Alignment Target
Number of Employees
14,000
13,000
12,000
11,000
10,000
12,677
11,503
11,229 (8-16-97)
10,874
10,613
10,269
Apr. 95
Oct. 95
Oct. 96
Apr. 97
Oct. 97
Oct. 98
Oct. 99
Oct. 2000

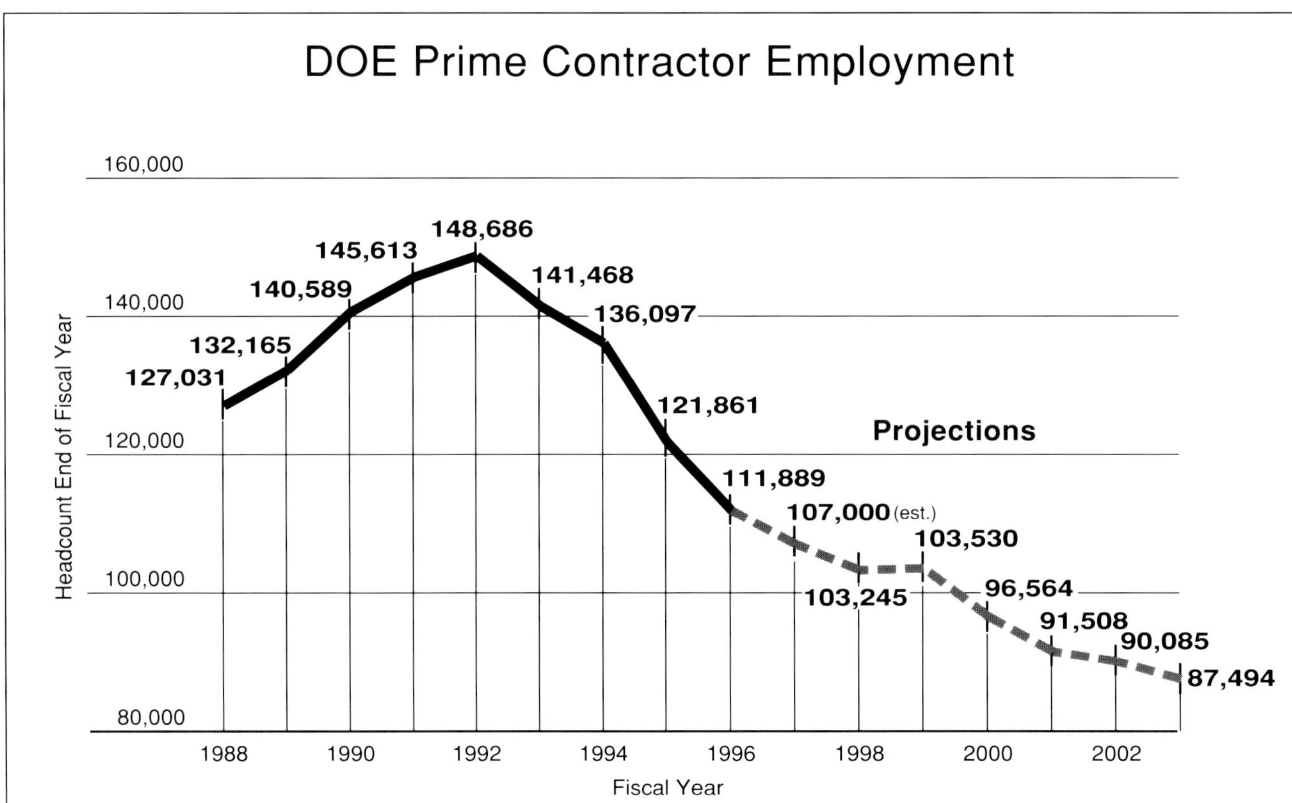
DOE Prime Contractor Employment
Headcount End of Fiscal Year
160,000
140,000
120,000
100,000
80,000
127,031
132,165
140,589
145,613
148,686
141,468
136,097
121,861
111,889
107,000 (est.)
103,245
103,530
96,564
91,508
90,085
87,494
Projections
1988
1990
1992
1994
1996
1998
2000
2002
Fiscal Year

through staff aging and attrition will need to be minimized. Construction of the National Ignition Facility and the Dual-Axis Radiographic Hydrodynamic Test Facility will provide new experimental test capabilities. Additionally, a source for tritium will be needed to provide an adequate supply for the enduring nuclear weapon stockpile. New facilities will be required to disassemble and convert surplus plutonium pits and fabricate mixed oxide fuel for burning in existing commercial reactors. Existing or planned high level waste vitrification facilities, coupled with new material preparation facilities, will be required to immobilize surplus weapons plutonium. Modifications to existing or planned facilities will be utilized for the long-term storage of surplus fissile materials. Adequate funding will also need to be made available to support Naval Nuclear Propulsion Program development efforts.

The Environmental Quality cleanup goals and objectives reflect the pressing need to reduce spending in the short term, while reducing both economic and environmental liabilities in the long term. Achievement of the accelerated environmental cleanup goals and objectives is dependent upon receiving stable funding at about the current funding level. In addition, accomplishment of these goals and objectives depends upon effective implementation of a wide array of management initiatives designed to substantially reduce life-cycle costs, improve processes, and enhance performance. These initiatives include reducing support costs, creating the right incentives through performance-based contracting, optimizing project sequencing to reduce fixed costs, privatization and use of private-sector technology and experience, deployment of innovative technology, and benchmarking for process improvement. With regard to civilian radioactive waste, if legislation authorizing interim storage is enacted, substantial additional funding will be required for site-specific construction and procurement of waste acceptance and transportation equipment and services.

In order to meet the Nation's needs for cutting-edge science, DOE will have to periodically replace or make major upgrades to aging and/or outdated major experimental facilities. These needs will be weighed against the benefits from cost-effective modifications to existing facilities to ensure that the maximum national benefits are derived from existing infrastructure—this recognizes, however, that many of these science facilities have a finite useful life. The Secretary of Energy's Advisory Board has been asked to examine the long-term needs for advanced scientific research facilities to accomplish DOE's Science and Technology objectives.

Key External Factors

Although DOE's goals and objectives reflect unique roles and responsibilities, success will depend upon closely coordinated planning and the continuation of working relationships with a number of Federal agencies, State and local governments, Tribal Nations, private industry, and Congress.

It is especially important to recognize the complementary role other Federal agencies play in our energy, defense, environmental, and science programs. The strong interplay between energy, the environment, and global economics establishes links between the Department and the Environmental Protection Agency, Nuclear Regulatory Commission, NASA, Agency for International Development, and the Departments of Agriculture, Commerce, Interior, Justice, State, Transportation, and Treasury. Our national security programs foster close relationships with the Departments of Defense and State, the Intelligence community, Defense Nuclear Agency, and National Security Council. Our science programs are carefully coordinated with the National Academy of Sciences, National Institutes of Health, National Science Foundation, NASA, White House Office of Science and Technology Policy, and Departments of Defense, Commerce, Education, and Transportation. Finally, our environmental quality programs directly interface with the Environmental Protection Agency and Nuclear Regulatory Commission.

While DOE's clearly defined, singular mission responsibilities and programs are well coordinated with appropriate other Federal agencies, there are some crosscutting government functions and initiatives that the Department participates in that are beyond the mission of any one agency. Government functions and responsibilities such as national security, global climate change, medical research, and science education draw upon the expertise and capabilities of numerous agencies that need to work together to meet these overarching, common goals. At times, it may appear that the programs within these Federal agencies are somewhat overlapping and possibly redundant, and in some cases this may be partially true. The challenge is to define the role and develop the programs within each participating agency that best use that agency's unique financial, human, and technical resources in a way that optimizes overall government performance. OMB and the White House Office of Science and Technology Policy play an important leadership role in coordinating these efforts. DOE's contribution to these crosscutting programs is founded upon the distinctive technical and scientific expertise and capabilities located within its laboratory system and facilities. The Department is committed to continue working closely with other Federal agencies and with OMB and Congress to ensure its programs provide critical and unique contributions to these crosscutting efforts.

In addition to the aforementioned coordination efforts, and the fact that this strategic plan was developed in consultation with the Congress, customers, and stakeholders, there are still factors external to DOE's full control that can influence our desired outcomes. These factors include:

- Climate change may prove to be one of the most important strategic energy drivers, especially if international agreements are reached that would require carbon emissions to be reduced to 1990 levels or lower during the next 15 to 25 years.
- A host of potential regulatory actions could require major additional reductions in energy-related emissions during the next decade, and some are expensive if compliance must depend on current technology and approaches.
- Without legislative relief, restructuring the electric utility retail market could adversely impact industry's investment in longer-term research, development, and demonstration of renewables and advanced, lower-emission fossil fuel and advanced nuclear power technologies.
- By 2015, 60 percent of the existing coal-fueled and 40 percent of the nuclear-powered electric generating plants will be 40 years old. It is not clear how long these plants can operate due to regulatory and economic issues.
- The President's Committee of Advisors on Science and Technology has been tasked to make recommendations on the FY 1999 and future energy research and development programs. Their recommendations may alter the Administration's energy research and development priorities

- The Department's Stockpile Stewardship and Management Program will depend on the outcome of the lawsuit involving its programmatic environmental impact statement.
- National Security objectives may be affected by any force structure changes required due to the ratification of START II or the adoption of START III.
- DOE's stewardship and management of the nuclear weapons stockpile is dependent upon the Department of Defense's future vision of stockpile requirements as reflected in the Nuclear Weapons Stockpile Memorandum/Plan.
- Progress in implementation of international treaties and agreements and progress in technology advances will be necessary for implementation of various nonproliferation and nuclear safety initiatives.
- Continued cooperation of the international community is critical to improve nuclear safety and prevent the spread of nuclear weapons of mass destruction capabilities worldwide.
- Resolution of technical, institutional, and cost issues, as well as agreement with Russia and other nations, will determine the timing and extent to which surplus weapons plutonium disposition takes place.
- The Department's ability to sell excess uranium and achieve savings is dependent on market conditions. The Secretary has a statutory responsibility to dispose of uranium stockpiles in a manner that does not adversely impact the mining, milling, and conversion industries.
- The Environmental Quality *2006 Plan* for accelerating cleanup of DOE's contaminated nuclear weapons production sites requires the involvement of and acceptance by the public.
- Successful negotiated agreements, compliance certifications, and/or permits with the Environmental Protection Agency, State regulatory agencies, and local stakeholders will determine site cleanup schedules.
- DOE's long-term stewardship at cleanup sites is dependent upon consultations with other Federal agencies, Congress, Tribal Nations, representatives of regulatory agencies, State and local authorities, and other stakeholders.
- Accomplishing DOE's environmental cleanup objectives assumes the availability of commercial options for radioactive and hazardous waste disposal.
- Legislation currently before the Congress and litigation by utilities and other parties could have a significant impact on the storage and disposal of spent nuclear fuel and high-level radioacive waste.
- Failure to adopt proposed revisions to 10 CFR Part 960 will impair the process for evaluating the suitability of the permanent storage site for civilian radioactive waste.
- A revised Environmental Protection Agency radiological protection standard specific to the Yucca Mountain site is a prerequisite to getting a Nuclear Regulatory Commission license for permanent storage of civilian radioactive waste.
- International collaboration on large, expensive exploratory science efforts will become necessary and desirable as few countries will be able to afford such major commitments alone.
- Government support for basic research will remain strong, government support in technology commercialization will remain controversial.
- To meet the Nation's need for an informed and educated citizenry and to ensure the next generation of U.S. scientists, will re-

quire government, industry, and educators working as a team.

- The Army Corps of Engineers may be directed through DOE's FY 1998 appropriations legislation to review the Department's line item projects which could affect the planning and execution of as many as 68 of them.

While these external factors may represent challenges for the Department and the Nation, we also recognize that by effectively working together, we can be successful in achieving our collective goals.

Role of Program Evaluation

DOE uses program evaluations to measure and evaluate the progress of its goals and objectives, to identify issues, to adjust plans, and to determine the worthiness of proposed future efforts. Program evaluations are conducted *by* DOE for its own benefit and *for* DOE by external organizations and groups. One of the major program evaluations conducted by DOE is the ongoing evaluation of progress against the annual Performance Agreements between the Secretary and the President. Building upon DOE's April 1994 Strategic Plan, the Department has been developing, executing, and evaluating these performance plans since FY 1995. These efforts have provided valuable experience in developing commitments and evaluating the Department's progress on strategic goals.

In addition to these evaluations, DOE has commissioned program evaluations by "blue-ribbon" panels. In January 1994, a one-year effort was established to evaluate the Department's laboratory system. The Task Force on Alternative Futures for the Department's National Laboratories, chaired by Robert Galvin, the Chairman of the Executive Committee of Motorola, Inc., evaluated the laboratory system and proposed ways to reduce their costs of doing business while sustaining their long record of scientific discovery and technological innovation. As a result of the Galvin task force report, the Department established the Laboratory Operations Board to oversee management reforms at the DOE laboratories. This Board has evaluated and recommended changes in the management of the Department's R&D programs, and is evaluating the mechanisms, such as peer review, used to assure quality in the Department's laboratory programs.

Another group, the Task Force on Strategic Energy Research and Development, chaired by Daniel Yergin, president of Cambridge Energy Research Associates, evaluated the Department's $1.8 billion portfolio of applied energy programs. Their June 1995 report also influenced the goal and objectives of the Science and Technology area.

Finally, an advisory committee on external regulation of nuclear facility safety, was headed by John Ahearne, a former chairman of the Nuclear Regulatory Commission, and by Gerald Scannell, President of the National Safety Council and former Assistant Secretary of Labor for Occupational Safety and Health. The committee's recommendations have been addressed in the Environmental Quality and Corporate Management areas.

To complement program evaluations conducted by DOE, many external organizations and individuals have provided program evaluations in the form of reviews, critiques, and advice on current and future programs. These organizations include the Office of Management and Budget, White House Office of Science and Technology Policy, Congress, General Accounting Office, Congressional Research Service, Congressional Budget Office,

Department of Defense, National Research Council, National Science Foundation, Council on Competitiveness, American Physical Society, Secretary of Energy Advisory Board, Environmental Protection Agency, Nuclear Waste Technical Review Board, Institute for Defense Analysis, Defense Nuclear Facilities Safety Board, National Academy of Public Administration, and Nuclear Regulatory Commission. In addition to these Federal groups, the Department formally invites and receives evaluations by State and local agencies, Tribal Nations, and local citizens at each of its sites throughout the Nation.

The Department of Energy is used to, and readily accepts, evaluations of its programs and performance. The evaluations received from all sources were considered in the development of the current strategic plan.

In accordance with the Department's Strategic Management System, program evaluations will continue to be part of the ongoing strategic planning and annual performance planning. Annual program evaluations are scheduled for the Fall of each year. These evaluations will include the review of annual performance plans and performance agreements, the status of delivery of results for the fiscal year, and guidance for development of plans for the next fiscal year. Adjustments to the Strategic Plan will be included in the Annual Performance Plan submitted with the budget.

APPENDIX A

Statutes and Other Authorities for DOE Objectives

This list is representative of the authorities available to the Department to carry out its activities.

ENERGY RESOURCES

Generally Applicable Statutes:

- **Department of Energy Organization Act** (DOE Act) (42 U.S.C. 7101, et seq.);
- **Energy Conservation and Production Act** (42 U.S.C. 6801, et seq.);
- **Energy Policy Act of 1992** (Pub. L. No. 102-486, 42 U.S.C. scattered sections);
- **Energy Policy and Conservation Act** (42 U.S.C. 6201, et seq.);
- **National Energy Conservation Policy Act** (42 U.S.C. 8201, et seq.);

Objective 1

Reduce the vulnerability of the U.S. economy to disruptions in energy supplies.

Statutes:

- **Chapter 641 of title 10, United States Code** (Naval Petroleum Reserves authority);
- **Energy Policy Act of 1992**
  - § 303-305 (42 U.S.C. 13212-13214) (alternative fuels for Federal Government use);
  - § 405-414 (42 U.S.C. 13231-13239) (alternative fuels for non-Federal use);
  - § 501-514 (42 U.S.C. 13251-13264) (replacement fuels, alternative fuels, and alternative fueled private vehicles);
  - § 601-626 (42 U.S.C. 13271-13296) (electric motor vehicles);
  - § 1203-1205, § 1211-1212 (42 U.S.C. 13312-13314, 13316-13317) (renewable energy);
  - § 1301-1341 (42 U.S.C. 13331-13370) (coal);
  - § 2001-2028 (42 U.S.C. 13401-13415, 13431-13438) (oil and gas supply enhancement and demand reduction);
  - § 2101-2126 (42 U.S.C. 13451-13495) (energy efficiency, renewable energy, and nuclear energy);
  - § 2101-2203, 2206 (42 U.S.C. 13501-13503, 13506) (energy efficiency and economic productivity);
- **Energy Policy and Conservation Act**
  - § 101-181 (42 U.S.C. 6211-6251) (domestic supply availability, including Strategic Petroleum Reserve authorities);
  - § 201-281 (42 U.S.C. 6261-6285) (standby energy authorities and international energy program);
- **Federal Power Act,** § 202 (16 U.S.C. 824a) (electricity export authority);
- **Federal Nonnuclear Energy Research and Development Act of 1974** (42 U.S.C. 5901-5920) (comprehensive nonnuclear research and development, including coal, oil, and natural gas programs);
- **National Defense Authorization Act for Fiscal Year 1996,** title 34 (Pub. L. No. 104-106) (sale of Naval Petroleum Reserve Numbered 1 and study of future of other Naval Petroleum Reserves);
- **National Energy Conservation Policy Act,**

- § 521-569 (42 U.S.C. 8241-8259, 8271-8278) (Federal energy initiative);
- § 801-804 (42 U.S.C. 8287-8287c) (energy savings performance contracts);

- **Natural Gas Act,** §3 (15 U.S.C. 717b) (exportation or importation of natural gas);
- **Natural Gas Policy Act of 1978,**
  - § 301-304 (15 U.S.C. 3361-3364) (emergency natural gas authority);
  - § 401-403 (15 U.S.C. 3391-3393) (natural gas curtailment policies);
- **Solar Energy Research, Development, and Demonstration Act of 1974** (42 U.S.C. 5551-5566) (research and development in solar technology);
- **Energy Supply and Environmental Coordination Act of 1974** (15 U.S.C. 791-798) (alternative fuels use by electric power plants);

Executive Orders:

- **Executive Order 12235** (delegates authority under §§ 302 and 303 of the Natural Gas Policy Act of 1978 to the Secretary of Energy);

Objective 2

Ensure that a competitive electricity generation industry is in place that can deliver adequate and affordable supplies with reduced environmental impact.

Statutes:

- **Atomic Energy Act of 1954,** § 31 (42 U.S.C. 2051) (research and development relating nuclear processes, atomic energy, and nuclear material);
- **DOE Act,**
  - § 102 (9) and (12) (42 U.S.C. 7112(9), (12)) (purposes of DOE — provision of adequate supply of energy at lowest reasonable cost and foster competition among parties engaged in the supply of energy)
  - § 203 (a) (1) (42 U.S.C. 7133(a)(1)) (assignment of duties related to management of electric power supply);
- **Energy Policy Act of 1992**
  - § 303-305 (42 U.S.C. 13212-13214) (alternative fuels for Federal Government use);
  - § 405-414 (42 U.S.C. 13231-13239) (alternative fuels for non-Federal use);
  - § 501-514 (42 U.S.C. 13251-13264) (replacement fuels, alternative fuels, and alternative fueled private vehicles);
  - § 601-626 (42 U.S.C. 13271-13296) (electric motor vehicles);
  - § 1203-1205, 1211-1212 (42 U.S.C. 13312-13314, 13316-13317) (renewable energy);
  - § 1301-1341 (42 U.S.C. 13331-13370) (coal);
  - § 2001-2028 (42 U.S.C. 13401-13415, 13431-13438) (oil and gas supply enhancement and demand reduction);
  - § 2101-2126 (42 U.S.C. 13451-13495) (energy efficiency, renewable energy, and nuclear energy);
  - § 2101-2203, 2206 (42 U.S.C. 13501-13503, 13506) (energy efficiency and economic productivity);
- **Federal Power Act,** § 202 (16 U.S.C. 824a) (electricity export authority);
- **Federal Nonnuclear Energy Research and Development Act of 1974** (42 U.S.C. 5901-5920) (comprehensive nonnuclear research and development, including coal, oil, and natural gas programs);

- **Natural Gas Act,** §3 (15 U.S.C. 717b) (exportation or importation of natural gas);
- **Natural Gas Policy Act of 1978,**
  - § 301-304 (15 U.S.C. 3361-3364) (emergency natural gas authority);
  - § 401-403 (15 U.S.C. 3391-3393) (natural gas curtailment policies);
- **Solar Energy Research, Development, and Demonstration Act of 1974** (42 U.S.C. 5551-5566) (research and development in solar technology);
- **Renewable Energy and Energy Efficiency Technology Competitiveness Act of 1989** (42 U.S.C. 12001-12007) (demonstration and deployment of renewable energy and energy efficiency technologies for buildings and transportation);
- **Energy Supply and Environmental Coordination Act of 1974** (15 U.S.C. 791-798) (alternative fuels use by electric power plants);
- **Bonneville Project Act of 1937** (16 U.S.C. 832-832*l*) (sale and disposition of electric energy generated at the Bonneville project);
- **Flood Control Act of 1944,** §5 (16 U.S.C. 825s) (authority to transmit and dispose of electric power and energy);
- **Reclamation Project Act of 1938,** §9 (c) (43 U.S.C. 485h (c) (Western Area Power Administration);
- **Department of the Interior and Related Agencies Appropriations Acts for Fiscal Years 1986-1995 and 1997** (Pub. L. Nos. 99-190, 99-591, 100-202, 100-446, 101-45, 101-121, 101-302, 101-512, 102-154, 102-381, 103-138, 103-332, 104-208) (clean coal technology);
- **Global Change Research Act of 1990** (15 U.S.C. 2921, et seq.) (interagency program to study and improve the understanding of and response to global change);
- **National Climate Program Act** (15 U.S.C. 2901-2908) (multi-agency program on the effects of climate on energy supply and demand, the natural environment, and other areas);

Objective 3

Reduce energy-related environmental impacts through more efficient energy use.

Statutes:

- **Atomic Energy Act of 1954**, § 31 (42 U.S.C. 2051) (research and development relating nuclear processes, atomic energy, and nuclear material);
- **National Energy Conservation Policy Act,**
  - § 521-569 (42 U.S.C. 8241-8259, 8271-8278) (Federal energy initiative);
  - § 801-804 (42 U.S.C. 8287-8287c) (energy savings performance contracts);
- **Energy Policy Act of 1992**
  - § 303-305 (42 U.S.C. 13212-13214) (alternative fuels for Federal Government use);
  - § 405-414 (42 U.S.C. 13231-13239) (alternative fuels for non-Federal use);
  - § 501-514 (42 U.S.C. 13251-13264) (replacement fuels, alternative fuels, and alternative fueled private vehicles);
  - § 601-626 (42 U.S.C. 13271-13296) (electric motor vehicles);
  - § 1203-1205, 1211-1212 (42 U.S.C. 13312-13314, 13316-13317) (renewable energy);
  - § 1301-1341 (42 U.S.C. 13331-13370) (coal);
  - § 2001-2028 (42 U.S.C. 13401-13415, 13431-13438) (oil and gas supply enhancement and demand reduction);
  - § 2101-2126 (42 U.S.C. 13451-13495) (energy efficiency, renewable energy, and nuclear energy);

  - § 2101-2203, 2206 (42 U.S.C. 13501-13503, 13506) (energy efficiency and economic productivity);
- **Department of Energy Metal Casting Competitiveness Research Act of 1990** (15 U.S.C. 5301, et seq.) (technology development for metals industry);
- **Department of the Interior and Related Agencies Appropriations Acts for Fiscal Years 1986-1995 and 1997** (Pub. L. Nos. 99-190, 99-591, 100-202, 100-446, 101-45, 101-121, 101-302, 101-512, 102-154, 102-381, 103-138, 103-332, 104-208) (clean coal technology);
- **Energy Policy and Conservation Act**
  - § 101-181 (42 U.S.C. 6211-6251) (domestic supply availability, including Strategic Petroleum Reserve authorities);
  - § 201-281 (42 U.S.C. 6261-6285) (standby energy authorities and international energy program);
- **Global Change Research Act of 1990** (15 U.S.C. 2921, et seq.) (interagency program to study and improve the understanding of and response to global change);
- **National Climate Program Act** (15 U.S.C. 2901-2908) (multi-agency program on the effects of climate on energy supply and demand, the natural environment, and other areas);
- **Renewable Energy and Energy Efficiency Technology Competitiveness Act of 1989** (42 U.S.C. 12001-12007) (demonstration and deployment of renewable energy and energy efficiency technologies for buildings and transportation);
- **Steel and Aluminum Energy Conservation and Technology Competitiveness Act of 1988** (15 U.S.C. 5101, et seq.) (R&D program to develop competitive manufacturing technologies and increase energy efficiency in the steel and aluminum industries);

Objective 4

Support U.S. energy, environmental, and economic interests in global markets.

Statutes:

- **DOE Act,**
  - § 102 (42 U.S.C. 7112) (purposes of the Department);
  - § 203(a)(1-4, 6-7, 9-10) (42 U.S.C. 7133(a) (1-4, 6-7, 9-10)) (functions assigned to assistant secretaries);
- **Energy Policy Act of 1992,**
  - § 1203-1204, 1211 (42 U.S.C.13312-13313, 13316) (renewable energy exports programs);
  - § 1331-1333, 1338 (42 U.S.C. 13361-13363, 13337) (coal export program):
  - § 1601-1609 (42 U.S.C. 13381-13388) (global climate change);
- **Support for East European Democracy Act of 1985**, § 502(f) (22 U.S.C. 5452(f)) (export of clean coal technology);
- **Global Change Research Act of 1990** (15 U.S.C. 2921, et seq.) (interagency program to study and improve the understanding of and response to global change);
- **National Climate Program Act** (15 U.S.C. 2901-2908) (multi-agency program on the effects of climate on energy supply and demand, the natural environment, and other areas);

Objective 5

Carry out information collection, analysis, and research that will facilitate development of informed positions on long-term energy supply and use alternatives.

Statutes:

- **DOE Act**,
  - § 102 (42 U.S.C. 7112) (purposes of the Department);
  - § 205 (42 U.S.C. 7135) (Energy Information Administration);
  - § 209 (42 U.S.C. 7139) (energy research office);
  - § 301-309 (42 U.S.C. 7151-7157) (transfer of functions);

NATIONAL SECURITY

Generally Applicable Statutes:

- **Department of Energy Organization Act (DOE Act),** § (42 U.S.C. 7101 et seq.);
- **Atomic Energy Act of 1954** (42 U.S.C. 2011 et seq.);
- **Soviet Nuclear Threat Reduction Act of 1991** (22 U.S.C. 2551 note);
- **Annual Department of Energy national security authorization Acts**, 1977 to present (since 1986, enacted as title XXXI of National Defense Authorization Acts);

Objective 1

Maintain confidence in the safety, reliability, and performance of the nuclear weapons stockpile without nuclear testing

Statutes

- **Atomic Energy Act of 1954**
  - § 25 (42 U.S.C. 2035) (establishes the Division of Military Application);
  - Chapter 4 (42 U.S.C. 2061-2064) (R&D in the theory and production of atomic energy, including application for military purposes);
  - Chapter 5 (42 U.S.C. 2071-2078) (production of special nuclear materials);
  - Chapter 9 (42 U.S.C. 2121-2123) (military application of atomic energy);
- **National Defense Authorization Act for Fiscal Year 1994**, §3138 (42 U.S.C. 2121 note) (establishes the Stockpile Stewardship Program);
- **National Defense Authorization Act for Fiscal Year 1996**, §3133 (42 U.S.C. 2121 note) (establishes a tritium production program capable of meeting the tritium requirements of the United States for nuclear weapons);

Objective 2

Replace nuclear testing with a science-based Stockpile Stewardship and Management Program

Statutes:

- **National Defense Authorization Act for Fiscal Year 1994,** §3138, (42 U.S.C. 2121 note); (establishes the Stockpile Stewardship Program);

Objective 3

Ensure the vitality of DOE's national security enterprise.

Statutes:

- **Atomic Energy Act of 1954**

  - Chapter 12 (42 U.S.C. 2161-2169) (control of Restricted Data and establishment of personnel security program)
  - Chapter 18 (42 U.S.C. 2271-2284) (criminal provisions relating to security functions)
  - § 161 (42 U.S.C. 2201) (protection of nuclear materials and Restricted Data);
- **Atomic Weapons and Special Nuclear Materials Rewards Act**, §§2-7 (50 U.S.C. 47a-47f) (rewards for information on illegal possession of atomic weapons or special nuclear material)
- **Defense Production Act of 1950** (50 U.S.C. App. 2061 et seq.) (conversion of civilian materials to military use);
- **Economic Espionage Act of 1996** (Pub.L. No. 104-294) (prevention of economic espionage);
- **National Defense Authorization Act for Fiscal Year 1993**, §§ 3161 and 3163 (42 U.S.C. 7274h, 7274j) (DOE defense nuclear facilities workforce restructuring plan);
- **National Defense Authorization Act for Fiscal Year 1995,** § 3131 (Pub.L. No. 103-337) (provides a "Stockpile Stewardship Recruitment and Training Program");
- **National Defense Authorization Act for Fiscal Year 1997**, § 1441 (Pub.L.No. 104-201) establishes National Coordinator on Nonproliferation (for weapons of mass destruction) and provides funding for cooperative plutonium disposition activities with Russia;

Executive Orders

- **Executive Order 10450** (security requirements for Government employment);
- **Executive Order 10865** (safeguarding classified information within industry);
- **Executive Order 11057** (communication of Restricted Data);
- **Executive Order 12958** (procedures for classification of national security information);
- **Executive Order 12968** (procedures for access to classified information);
- **Executive Order 12938** (national emergency in regards to weapons of mass destruction)

Emergency Planning and Operations

- **Executive Order 10480** (Defense Production Act priority contracting and allocation authority);
- **Executive Order 11912** (DPA priority contracting and allocation authority to maximize domestic energy supplies);
- **Executive Order 11953 and 12656** (emergency preparedness);
- **Executive Order 12742** (national security industrial responsiveness);

Intelligence

- **Executive Order 12333** (functions and responsibilities of U.S. intelligence community);
- **Executive Order 12334** (President's Intelligence Oversight Board);
- **Executive Order 12356** (special access programs for intelligence information);
- **Executive Order 12958**

Treaty

- **Open Skies Treaty**

Objective 4

Reduce nuclear weapons and materials stockpiles worldwide and dispose of excess weapons-usable fissile materials.

Statutes:

- **Soviet Nuclear Threat Reduction Act of 1991 ("Nunn-Lugar")** (22 U.S.C. 2551 note) authorizes the President to establish and conduct programs to assist the demilitarization of the independent states of the former Soviet Union. Programs include transporting , storing, safeguarding and destruction of nuclear and other weapons; and establishing verifiable safeguards against the proliferation of such weapons and their components. Amendments to the Soviet Nuclear Threat Reduction Act since 1991 have continued and expanded the authority of the President to assist states of the former Soviet Union with demilitarization, nonproliferation and arms control initiatives. These include the Freedom Support Act of 1992 (PL. 102-511); The Former Soviet Union Demilitarization Act of 1992 (Title XIV of the National Defense Authorization Act for Fiscal Year 1993, PL. 102-484, and Titles XIII-XV of the National Defense Authorization Act for Fiscal Year 1997, (PL. 104-201);
- **Department of Energy Organization Act,** § 212 (42 U.S.C. 7143) establishes the Office of Fissile Materials Disposition;
- **National Defense Authorization Act for Fiscal Year 1996,** § 3131 (Pub.L.No. 104-106), authorizes conduct of programs to improve fissile materials protection, control, and accountability in Russia;
- **United States Enrichment Corporation Privatization Act,** § 3112 (Pub.L.No. 104-134) establishes terms and conditions governing the disposition of surplus highly enriched uranium;
- **Export Administration Act** (Pub.L.No. 96-72 of 9-29-79 and Pub.L.No. 99-64 of 7-12-85 Part 778)

Objective 5

Continue leadership in policy support and technology development for international arms control and non-proliferation efforts.

Statutes:

- **Atomic Energy Act of 1954,** §§ 123-131 (42 U.S.C. 2153-2160) (international activities related to atomic energy);
- **FY 1994 Foreign Operations Appropriations Act,** § 560 (Pub.L.No. 103-87) (authorizes the Department to institute a program of cooperation between scientific and engineering institutes in the New Independent States of the Former Soviet Union and national laboratories and other qualified academic institutions in the United States);

Treaties:

- **Treaty on the Nonproliferation of Nuclear Weapons (NPT)**;
- **The Threshold Test Ban Treaty (TTBT)** (verification of compliance with treaty provisions by the parties);
- **Agreement for Cooperation between the United States of America and the International Atomic Energy Agency**
- **Agreement with the International Atomic Energy Agency for the Application of Safeguards in the United States of America with Protocol (U.S. - IAEA) Treaty for Safeguards in the U.S.** (Voluntary Offer);

Objective 6

Meet national security requirements for naval nuclear propulsion and for other advanced nuclear power systems.

Statutes:

- **Energy Reorganization Act of 1974**, § 104 (42 U.S.C. 5814) (naval reactors);
- **Department of Energy Organization Act**, § 309 (42 U.S.C. 7158) (naval reactors);
- **Department of Defense Authorization Act, 1985,** § 1634 (freezes E.O. 12344 on Naval Reactors in place unless changed by law) (42 U.S.C. 7158 note);
- **Energy Policy Act of 1992**, §§ 2121-2124 (42 U.S.C. 13491-13494) (advanced nuclear reactors R&D);

Objective 7

Improve international nuclear safety.

Statutes:

- **Department of Energy Organization Act,** § 102(10) (42 U.S.C. 7112(10)) authorizes DOE to undertake international energy activities, in coordination with the Secretary of State;
- **Energy Reorganization Act of 1974,** § 103(8) and 107(a) (42 U.S.C. 5813(8) and 5817(a)) DOE may encourage and participate in international cooperation in energy and related environmental research and development, and DOE may make arrangements for the conduct of research and development activities with private or public institutions, including participation in joint or cooperative projects of a research, developmental, or experimental nature;
- **Atomic Energy Act of 1954**, § 31 (42 U.S.C. 2051) of atomic energy research and development activities through contracts, agreements and loans with private or public institutions or persons, including foreign governments;
- **Soviet Nuclear Threat Reduction Act of 1991** and subsequent amendments (see Objective 4) provide authority for the transfer of certain funds to DOE for use in assisting in certain nuclear safety activities in the independent states of the former Soviet Union;

ENVIRONMENTAL QUALITY

Generally Applicable Statutes:

- **Department of Energy Organization Act,** §102(11), (13), and (15) (42 U.S.C. 7112(11), (13), and (15)) and §203(a)(3) and (8) (42 U.S.C. 7133(a)(3) and (8));
- **Atomic Energy Act of 1954**, §161 b. and i. (42 U.S.C. 2201(b) and (I));
- **Comprehensive Environmental Response, Compensation, and Liability Act of 1980**, (42 U.S.C. 9601 et seq.);
- **Solid Waste Disposal Act (RCRA)** (42 U.S.C. 6901 et seq.);
- **National Environmental Policy Act of 1969** (42 U.S.C. 4321 et seq.);
- **Clean Air Act** (42 U.S.C. 7401 et seq.);
- **Federal Water Pollution Control Act** (Clean Water Act) (33 U.S.C. 1251 et seq.);
- **Safe Drinking Water Act** (42 U.S.C. 300f et seq.);
- **Toxic Substances Control Act** (15 U.S.C. 2601 et seq.);
- **Hazardous Materials Transportation Act** (49 U.S.C. 5101 et seq.);

Objective 1

Reduce the most serious risks from the environmental legacy of the U.S. nuclear weapons complex first.

Statutes:

- **Comprehensive Environmental Response, Compensation, and Liability Act of 1980** (42 U.S.C. 9601 et seq.) (cleanup of contaminated sites);
- **Solid Waste Disposal Act** (42 U.S.C. 6901 et seq.) (minimization of generation of hazardous waste, hazardous waste management, and cleanup of past contamination at currently active sites);
- **National Defense Authorization Act for Fiscal Years 1992 and 1993**, § 3135 (42 U.S.C. 7274g) (environmental restoration and waste management five-year plan and budget reports);
- **National Defense Authorization Act for Fiscal Year 1994**, § 3153 (42 U.S.C. 7274k) (baseline environmental management reports);

Objective 2

Clean up as many as possible of the Department's 83 remaining contaminated geographic sites by 2006.

Statutes:

- **Comprehensive Environmental Response, Compensation, and Liability Act of 1980** (42 U.S.C. 9601 et seq.) (cleanup of contaminated sites);
- **Solid Waste Disposal Act** (42 U.S.C. 6901 et seq.) (minimization of generation of hazardous waste, hazardous waste management, and cleanup of past contamination at currently active sites);
- **National Defense Authorization Act for Fiscal Years 1992 and 1993**, § 3135 (42 U.S.C. 7274g) (environmental restoration and waste management five-year plan and budget reports);
- **National Defense Authorization Act for Fiscal Year 1996**, §3156 (42 U.S.C. 7274k note) (accelerated schedule for environmental restoration and waste management activities);
- **National Defense Authorization Act for Fiscal Year 1997**, § 3143 (42 U.S.C. 7274n) (program of closure-acceleration projects);
- **Uranium Mill Tailings Radiation Control Act of 1978** (42 U.S.C. 7901 et seq.) (program to clean up inactive uranium milling sites and other contaminated properties in their vicinity);

Objective 3

Safely and expeditiously dispose of waste generated by nuclear weapons and civilian nuclear research and development programs and make defense high-level radioactive wastes disposal-ready.

Statutes:

- **Department of Energy National Security and Military Applications of Nuclear Energy Authorization Act of 1980,** §213, Pub.L.No. 96-164 (establishes WIPP);
- **Waste Isolation Pilot Plant Land Withdrawal Act** (Pub.L.No. 102-579) (withdraws land for WIPP and establishes procedures for starting its operation);
- **National Defense Authorization Act for Fiscal Years 1990 and 1991**, § 3141 (42 U.S.C. 7274a) (defense waste cleanup technology program);

- **Energy Policy Act of 1992**, § 2113 (42 U.S.C. 13473) (plan for developing new technologies for minimizing the volume and toxic lifetime of nuclear waste);

Objective 4

Prevent future pollution.

Statutes:

- **Solid Waste Disposal Act** (42 U.S.C. 6901 et seq.) (minimization of generation of hazardous waste, hazardous waste management, and cleanup of past contamination at currently active sites);
- **Energy Policy Act of 1992**, § 2113 (42 U.S.C. 13473) (plan for developing new technologies for minimizing the volume and toxic lifetime of nuclear waste;

Objective 5

Dispose of high-level radioactive waste and spent nuclear fuel in accordance with the Nuclear Waste Policy Act as amended.

Statutes:

- **Nuclear Waste Policy Act of 1982** (42 U.S.C. 10101 et seq.) (disposal, interim storage, monitored retrievable storage and transportation of high-level radioactive waste and spent nuclear fuel);

Objective 6

Reduce the life-cycle costs of environmental cleanup.

Statutes:

- **National Defense Authorization Act for Fiscal Years 1990 and 1991**, § 3141 (42 U.S.C. 7274a) (defense waste cleanup technology program);
- **National Defense Authorization Act for Fiscal Year 1997**, § 3143 (42 U.S.C. 7274n) (program of closure-acceleration projects) §§ 3171-3180 (42 U.S.C. 7274k note) (cost effective management mechanisms, innovative technologies, and performance-based contracting);
- **Energy Policy Act of 1992**, § 2113 (42 U.S.C. 13473) (plan for developing new technologies for minimizing the volume and toxic lifetime of nuclear waste);

Objective 7

Maximize the beneficial reuse of land and effectively control risks from residual contamination.

Statutes:

- National Defense Authorization Act for Fiscal Year 1997, §3153 (42 U.S.C. 7274k note) (future use plans for defense nuclear facilities at which environmental restoration and waste management activities are occurring);

SCIENCE AND TECHNOLOGY

Generally Applicable Statutes:

- **Department of Energy Organization Act (DOE Act)** (42 U.S.C. 7101 et seq.);
- **Atomic Energy Act of 1954** (42 U.S.C. 2011 et seq.);
- **Energy Reorganization Act of 1974** (42 U.S.C. 5801 et seq.);
- **Federal Nonnuclear Energy Research and Development Act of 1974** (42 U.S.C. 5901 et seq.);

Objective 1

Develop the science that underlies DOE's long-term mission

Statutes:

- **Atomic Energy Act of 1954**
  - § 31 (42 U.S.C. 2051) (research and development (R&D) related to: (1) nuclear processes, theory, and production, and (2) use of nuclear and radioactive materials for medical, biological, agricultural, health, and industrial purposes);
  - § 32 (42 U.S.C. 2052) (conducting energy-related R&D activities in DOE facilities, e.g., National Laboratories);
  - § 33 (42 U.S.C. 2053) (Energy R&D for non-DOE entities if private facilities inadequate);
  - § 91 (42 U.S.C. 2121) (R&D in the military applications of atomic weapons and the production of atomic weapons and atomic weapons parts);
- **DOE Act**
  - § 102(5) and (6) (42 U.S.C. 7112(5), (6)) (carry out a comprehensive energy R&D program);
  - § 203(a)(2) and (3) (42 U.S.C. 7133(a)(2), (3)) (R&D in solar, geothermal, recycling, fossil, and nuclear energy and environmental effects of energy technologies);
  - § 209 (42 U.S.C. 7139) (creates Office of Energy Research to: (1) advise the Secretary on R&D programs, R&D financial assistance, and lab management other than nuclear weapons labs, and (2) supervise DOE R&D activities);
  - § 301 (42 U.S.C. 7151) (transferred Energy Research and Development Administration functions and Energy Reorganization Act of 1974 functions to DOE);
- **Energy Reorganization Act of 1974**, § 103 (42 U.S.C. 5813) (management of R&D programs respecting all energy sources; energy-related environmental, biomedical, and physical science R&D; international R&D cooperation);
- **Federal Nonnuclear Energy Research and Development Act of 1974**, §§ 4 and 8 (42 U.S.C. 5903, 5907) (energy R&D&D, including coal, oil, natural gas, and other nonnuclear programs);
- **High-Performance Computing Act of 1991**, § 203 (15 U.S.C. 5523) (high-performance computing and communications systems R&D);
- **Spark M. Matsunaga Hydrogen Research, Development, and Demonstration Act of 1990** (42 U.S.C. 12401-12408) (RD&D concerning hydrogen as an economic fuel or storage medium);
- **National Defense Authorization Act for Fiscal Year 1991**, § 1801 (sections 2901-2904, title 10, United States Code) (environmental R&D to meet DOD and DOE environmental obligations);
- **National Defense Authorization Act for Fiscal Years 1990 and 1991**, § 3141 (42 U.S.C. 7274a) (defense waste cleanup technology program);
- **National Superconductivity and Competitiveness Act of 1988**, § 4 (15 U.S.C. 5203) (DOE superconductivity research and development activities);

Objective 2

Deliver leading-edge technologies that are critical to the DOE mission and the Nation.

Statutes:

- **Atomic Energy Act of 1954**
  - §§ 151-160 (42 U.S.C. 2181-2190) (patents and inventions relating to nonmilitary utilization; prior art; licenses, royalties, Federally financed research, etc.);
  - §§ 141-149 (42 U.S.C. 2161-2169) (control of information);
- **Energy Reorganization Act of 1974**, § 107(e) (42 U.S.C. 5817(e)) (dissemination of research results).;
- **Department of Energy Organization Act**, § 102(5)(D) (42 U.S.C. 7112(5)(D)) (disseminate information resulting from R&D programs);
- **Federal Nonnuclear Research and Development Act of 1974**, §§ 7 and 8 (42 U.S.C. 5906, 5907) (demonstrations of new energy technology and patent policy);
- **Stevenson-Wydler Technology Innovation Act of 1980** (15 U.S.C. 3701 et seq.) (amended numerous times) (authorizes government-owned, contractor operated (GOCO) labs to enter into cooperative research and development agreements (CRADAs) with non-Federal parties; establishes other aspects of the technology development relationship between GOCO laboratory contractors and DOE, such as title to inventions; requires Offices of Research and Technology Application at major labs to coordinate activities; and requires making federally-funded R&D more accessible to State and local governments and private industry);
- **National Competitiveness Technology Transfer Act of 1989** (section 3131(d) of the National Defense Authorization Act for Fiscal Years 1990 and 1991) (15 U.S.C. 3710a, note) (technology transfer and CRADAs for GOCO labs);
- **Bayh-Dole Act of 1980** (35 U.S.C. 200 et seq.) (small businesses and nonprofit organizations retain title to inventions made under funding agreements with DOE; Federal agencies grant exclusive licenses);
- **Energy Policy Act of 1992**
  - § 1211 (42 U.S.C. 13316) (renewable energy international technology transfer program with AID);
  - § 1332 (42 U.S.C. 13362) (clean coal international technology program with AID);
  - § 1608 (42 U.S.C. 13387) (innovative environmental international technology transfer program with AID);
  - §§ 2011-2014 (42 U.S.C. 13411-13414) (enhanced oil recovery, oil shale, natural gas supply, and natural gas end-use technologies R&D programs);
  - § 2025 (42 U.S.C. 13435) (R&D on electric motor vehicles and associated equipment);
  - §§ 2201 and 2202 (42 U.S.C. 13501-13502) (National Advanced Materials Initiative and National Advanced Manufacturing Technologies Initiative);
  - § 2203 (42 U.S.C. 13503) (supporting research and technical analysis);
  - §§ 3001-3002 (42 U.S.C. 13541-13542) (procedures and forms of agreement for carrying out RD&D and commercialization activities under EPACT);
  - §§ 611-616 (42 U.S.C. 13281-86) (electric and hybrid motor vehicle commercial demonstration program);
- **High-Performance Computing Act of 1991**
  - § 102 (15 U.S.C. 5512) (National Research and Education Network);
  - § 203 (15 U.S.C. 5523) (DOE R&D and technology transfer on high-performance computing and communications systems);

- **National Cooperative Research and Production Act of 1993** (15 U.S.C. 4301 et seq.) (details exception to anti-trust prohibition against joint ventures in research and related activities by competitors) ;
- **Steel and Aluminum Energy Conservation and Technology Competitiveness Act of 1988** (15 U.S.C. 5101 et seq.); (R&D program to develop competitive manufacturing technologies and increase energy efficiency in the steel and aluminum industries);
- **Department of Energy Metal Casting Competitiveness Research Act of 1990** (15 U.S.C. 5301 et seq.) (technology development for metals industry);
- **National Defense Authorization Act for Fiscal Years 1988 and 1989,** §§ 3141-3151 (15 U.S.C. 4621-4631)) (DOE semi-conductor technology research excellence initiative);
- **Global Change Research Act of 1990** (15 U.S.C. 2921 et seq.), (interagency program to study and improve the understanding of and response to global change);
- **National Climate Program Act** (15 U.S.C. 2901-2908) (multi-agency program on the effects of climate on energy supply and demand, the natural environment, and other areas);
- **Solar Energy Research, Development, and Demonstration Act of 1974** (42 U.S.C. 5551-5566) (research and development in solar technology);
- **Renewable Energy and Energy Efficiency Technology Competitiveness Act of 1989** (42 U.S.C. 12001-12007) (demonstration and deployment of renewable energy and energy efficiency technologies for buildings and transportation);

Executive Orders:

- **E.O. 12591** and **E.O. 12618** (April 10 and December 22, 1987) Federal Technology Transfer Act implementation; labs assistance to universities and private sector; consultation on CRADAs and licensing agreements with foreign persons or organizations);

Objective 3

Improve the management of DOE's research enterprise to enhance the delivery of leading-edge science and technology at reduced costs.

Statutes:

- **Atomic Energy Act of 1954**
  - § 31 (42 U.S.C. 2051) (conducting R&D and training activities in nuclear energy and related fields);
  - § 32 (42 U.S.C. 2052) (conducting energy-related R&D activities in DOE facilities, including the National Laboratories);
  - § 33 (42 U.S.C. 2053) (conducting energy research and development activities for non-DOE entities);
  - § 161 g. and j. (42 U.S.C. 2201(g) and (j)) (acquiring and disposing of real and personal property);
- **DOE Act,**
  - § 209(b)(3) (42 U.S.C. 7139(b)(3)) (management of non-defense multi-purpose laboratories),
  - §§ 647-649 (42 U.S.C. 7257-7259) (acquisition, maintenance, construction, and use of laboratories and other facilities);
- **Energy Policy Act of 1992**, § 2203 (42 U.S.C. 13503) (construction of user facilities; policy and plans for multi-program energy laboratories);

- **Energy Reorganization Act of 1974**, §107 (42 U.S.C. 5817) (facilities and property)
- **National Defense Authorization Act for Fiscal Year 1991**, §3132 (42 U.S.C. 7257a) (GOCO labs R&D);
- **High-Performance Computing Act of 1991**
  - § 102 (15 U.S.C. 5512) (National Research and Education Network, communication among scientists);
  - § 203 (15 U.S.C. 5523) (DOE high-performance computing and communications systems R&D);
- **Federal Nonnuclear Energy Research and Development Act of 1974,** §§ 4 and 7 (42 U.S.C. 5903, 5906) (energy R&D through contracts and financial assistance, national laboratories, and working with the private sector);
- **National Superconductivity and Competitiveness Act**, §4 (15 U.S.C. 5203) (superconductivity R&D, including the management of property developed or made at the National Laboratories)

Executive Orders:

- **E.O. 12591** and **E.O. 12618** (labs assistance to universities and private sector);

Objective 4

Assist in the government-wide effort to advance the Nation's science education and literacy.

Statutes:

- **Atomic Energy Act of 1954**, § 31 b. (42 U.S.C. 2051(b)) (grants for education activities in relation to certain fields of nuclear theory and processes);
- **Department of Energy Organization Act**
  - § 102(19) (42 U.S.C. 7112(19) (support science education);
  - § 209(b)(4) (42 U.S.C. 7139(b)(4)) (the Director of Energy Research is responsible for advising the Secretary on education and training to support basic science);
- **Department of Energy Science Education Enhancement Act** (42 U.S.C. 7381 et seq.) (DOE involvement in mathematics, science and engineering education; establishes DOE partnerships with educational institutions).
- **Energy Policy Act of 1992**
  - § 2203(b) (42 U.S.C. 13503(b) (university and science education);
  - § 2204 (42 U.S.C. 13504) (math and science education);
- **Energy Reorganization Act of 1974**, §§ 103, 104, and 107 (42 U.S.C. 5813, 5814, 5817) (energy-related education and training and public dissemination of research results);
- **Electronic Freedom of Information Act Amendments of 1996** (Pub. L. No. 104-231) (5 U.S.C. 552) (facilitates electronic transfer of information to and from Federal agencies and the public);
- **High-Performance Computing Act of 1991**, § 102 (15 U.S.C. 5512) (National Research and Education Network);
- **Albert Einstein Distinguished Educator Fellowship Act of 1994** (42 U.S.C. 7382-7382f) (establishes within DOE a national fellowship program for elementary and secondary school mathematics and science teachers);

CORPORATE MANAGEMENT

Generally Applicable Statutes:

- **Department of Energy Organization Act (DOE Act)** (42 U.S.C. 7101 et seq.);
- **Atomic Energy Act of 1954** (42 U.S.C. 2011 et seq.);
- **Numerous statutes of Government-wide application, such as Federal Property and Administrative Services Act of 1949; chapters 11-91 of title 5, United States Code; Freedom of Information Act; Government Performance and Results Act of 1993; Chief Financial Officer Act of 1990; National Environmental Policy Act of 1969; Administrative Dispute Resolutions Act; and Information Technology Management Reform Act of 1996;**

Objective 1

Ensure the safety and health of the DOE workforce and members of the public, and the protection of the environment in all Departmental activities.

Statutes:

- **Atomic Energy Act of 1954**, §161 b. and i. (42 U.S.C. 2201(b) and (i)) (protect health and safety);
- **DOE Act**, § 102(13) (42 U.S.C. 7112(15)) (assure incorporation of national environmental protection goals in formulation and implementation of energy programs);
- **Defense Authorization Act for Fiscal Year 1993**, §§ 3162-3163 (42 U.S.C. 7274i-7274j) (medical evaluation of current and former DOE employees);

Objective 2

As a good neighbor and public partner, continually work with customers and stakeholders in an open, frank, and constructive manner.

Statutes:

- **DOE Act,** § 102(11) and (15) (42 U.S.C. 7112(11), (15)) (provision for DOE cooperation with State and local governments and for public participation in the development of national energy programs);
- **National Defense Authorization Act for Fiscal Year 1997**, § 3153 and § 3173(b)(3) (42 U.S.C. 7274k note) (citizen advisory board for each facility at which environmental restoration and waste management activities are occurring and consultation with the advisory board and the State before making certain decisions);
- **Atomic Energy Act of 1954,** §§ 141-148 (42 U.S.C. 2161-2168) (control, classification, and declassification of information);

Executive Order:

- **Executive Order 12862** (September 11, 1993) (setting customer service standards for Federal agencies);

Objective 3

Use efficient and effective corporate management systems and approaches to guide decision making, streamline and improve operations, align resources and reduce costs, improve the delivery of products and services, and evaluate performance.

Statutes:

- **DOE Act**
  - §102(2) and (3) (42 U.S.C. 7112(2), (3)) (provision for effective management of energy functions of the Federal Government and for a mechanism for coordinating national energy policy;
  - § 643 (42 U.S.C. 7253) (authority to organize and reorganize offices within DOE);
  - § 646 (42 U.S.C. 7256) (contracting authority);
  - § 650 (42 U.S.C. 7260) (authority to establish and alter field offices);
  - § 653 (42 U.S.C. 7263) (working capital fund);
- **Energy Policy Act of 1992**, § 2304 (42 U.S.C. 13523) (management plan for the conduct of research, development, demonstration, and commercial application of energy technologies);
- **Atomic Energy Act of 1954** (42 U.S.C. 2011 et seq.) (contracting authority);
- **Government Performance and Results Act of 1993** (§ 306 of title 5, United States Code, and §§ 1105(a)(29), 1115-1119, and 9703 of title 31, United States Code);
- **National Defense Authorization Act of 1993**, § 3161 (42 U.S.C. 7274h) (assisting communities near DOE sites and released DOE workers);
- **Clinger -Cohen Act of 1996** (40 U.S.C. 1401 et seq.) (Information Technology Management)